# The French Intelligence

The Yellow Vests, the CNCTR and G10 Commissions and the EU Next Frontier for Intelligence

# The French Intelligence

The Yellow Vests, the CNCTR and G10 Commissions and the EU Next Frontier for Intelligence

## Musa Khan Jalalzai

Vij Books

New Delhi (India)

*Published by*

**Vij Books**
*(An imprint of Vij Books India Pvt Ltd)*

(Publishers, Distributors & Importers)
4836/24, Ansari Road
Delhi – 110 002
Phone: 91-11-43596460
Mobile: 98110 94883
e-mail: contact@vijpublishing.com
www.vijbooks.in

ISBN: 978-81-19438-46-4  (Hardback)
ISBN: 978-81-19438-82-2  (Paperback)

# Contents

# Introduction

The Yellow Vests, Pension Reforms and the surge of radicalization and extremism in France prompted dozens of national security challenges. There have been speculations that with the interference of some neighbouring states, these protests became violent and challenged the authority of the state and law enforcement agencies. I have studied in detail all these abruptly emerged radicalised protests and economic terrorism that threatened France's political and economic integration by transporting their extremists, radicalized elements and foreign spies from Africa, South Asia and Some states in Europe. In 2019, the Yellow Vests protests exposed the difficult living conditions of citizens in France, which was hijacked by these forces. The recent violent protest (2023) also prompted several domestic security challenges by diverting the attention of French politicians and the international community toward their planning and activities. The Yellow Vests movement remained independent in its composition and demands. In its network, the movement brought together lower-middle class citizens dissatisfied with political representation and the establishment. In January 2008, in the office of the French President, Nicolas Sarkozy, a meeting took place, in which he highlighted the issue of Internet surveillance. Since the 1980s, French secret agencies have managed to develop modern communication intelligence capabilities, developed professional capabilities in the 2000s, while the threat posed by the Islamic State and domestic radicalized groups, which resulted in the Paris attacks in January 2015, a ground was prepared for the intelligence act, the most extensive piece of legislation ever adopted in France to regulate the work of intelligence agencies.

France has entered a political, social and economic transformation phase. The Niger crisis and military takeover has deeply disturbed the political and military leadership of the country, and the arrival of Wagner militia and other stakeholders on Niger soil caused a threatening security environment. In all these and other events, French intelligence exhibited its professional approach and proved that a strong and reformed secret agency can better manage national security crises. In fact, secret agencies in France has been a functional tool in the hands of the decision-maker, but later on they realized the importance of intelligence infrastructure. Persistent intelligence and security sector reforms were in fact, the reorganization and reinvention of French security infrastructure. As France has been a strong colonial power, its agencies have also been struggling to adopt modern intelligence tactics. French reform is based on the action of an attempt to explain or justify behaviour or an attitude of secret agencies with logical reasons, or a mechanism in which apparent logical reasons are given to justify behaviour. The government and the state have decided to modernise and centralise secret agencies. Expert and writer Anne Lise Michelot (Reform of the French Intelligence Oversight System-30 November 2028) has documented some aspects of the French intelligence oversight and reform:

"French intelligence remains a very secretive world from the public view, and the little presence it occupies in the press or public debate is more often than not one of scandal, abuse or failure. In 2008, the government initiated a reform process of the intelligence organisation, and continued in 2015, following the numerous terrorist attacks on the national territory. The result of this long process of reshaping the intelligence community has included attempts at perfecting and in some cases creating, oversight mechanisms. These reforms have been the subject of public and parliamentary debates for the past decade, as many politicians, scholars and journalists pointed out the lack of supervision and the relative freedom intelligence agencies enjoyed in performing their activities. Today, the French oversight system comprises a specific institution for each type of control. This diversified/ plural system was completed with the creation of a new institution, the Commission Nationale de Contrôle des Techniques de Renseignement, CNCTR (national commission for the control of intelligence techniques) in 2015. The creation of the CNCTR in 2015 to oversee the usage of intelligence techniques has attempted to bring France up to high democratic standards in terms of intelligence oversight. However, the commission's limited means hinder its ability to perform fully its duties."[1]

After these reforms, the threat of terrorism decreased but the threat of foreign spying exponentially exacerbated. Foreign spies attempted on many occasions to create civil unrest and infiltrate their spies into the system of the country. The Yellow Vest and the recent civil disobedience and terrorism, in which terrorist groups of all EU member states, illegal extremists and terrorists, Pakistani, Afghan and African looters demonstrated their power in France's cities and towns and that was a golden opportunity they established their networks on improvised bases. They transported their spies and intelligence units-adorned with military grade weapons to the cities and towns of France. In an interview with Le Monde newspaper, the head of (Nicolas Lerner has been director general of the Directorate General of Internal Security (DGSI) France's domestic intelligence agency described the country's potential security threats.

A series of coordinated terrorist attacks on 13 November 2015 in France killed 130 innocent citizens. Former President Francois Hollande described the attacks as an "act of war" organised by extremist elements. France has been living through an unshakeable ordeal as a powerful and humanist state since 2015. White jihad and White Supremacist groups, Muslim radicalized organizations from South Asia, Africa and Afghanistan have established their roots in French Society. They feel disconnected from society as well as socioeconomic and political systems. The French police and secret agencies are no doubt competent forces-fighting these evil forces, but with the arrival of jihadist and extremist elements from Pakistan, Africa and Middle East, engagement and work of law enforcement agencies aggravated and magnified. In 2023, President Macron's government experienced two violent protests, (2020 and 2023) in which extremist forces demonstrated and translated their anger violently. In 2023, terrorists and extremists jointly looted and set fire to government installations and public properties across the country. Protests were centred on Pension Reforms, while the agenda was different. Foreign spy agencies were clandestinely supporting them in case of military grade weapons, knives and masks. After these protests, revolts and mutinies in Africa emerged-coup d'etat were organized and French colonies were provoked to demand their rights.

In 2013, the Snowden revelations emotionally and mentally disturbed western world and pushed French policy makers to secure and expand the surveillance capabilities of their agencies through intelligence reform. On July 18 2023, French lawmakers and policy makers adopted a 'sweeping justice reform bill that includes a provision to allow law enforcement agents to remotely tap into the cameras, microphones and location services of phones and other internet-connected devices of some suspected criminals', Le Monde reported. Investigatory Power Law already existed and was in operation. Human Rights Watch, on 11 April 2020, criticised stop and search laws in France. Some national and international circles noted these illegal practices. The French state authorities were criticised on several occasions by domestic courts for the widespread practice of ethnic profiling during police stops. Human Rights Watch noted six associations

3

(Amnesty International France, Human Rights Watch, and MCDS, Open society Justice Initiative, Pazapas Belleville, and REAJI) on 22 July 2021, and filed petitions with the council of states. Expert and writer, Davide Basso (Macron promises to boost police as doubts over methods rise-10 June 2022, Euractiv) has noted that violence has shaken the country while Interior Minister Gérald Darmanin attempted to defend the government's law and order doctrine.

The Council of Europe sternly criticised excessive use of police force against the looters and extremist elements, but experts viewed it as financial terrorism. On 24 March 2023, Le Monde newspaper reported commissioner for human rights Dunja Mijatovic said that in the violent incidents some targeted the police. "But the sporadic acts of violence of some protesters or other reprehensible acts committed by other persons during a protest cannot justify excessive use of force by agents of the state. These acts are also not enough to deprive peaceful protesters of their right to freedom of assembly," Le Monde reported. However, the newspaper reported remarks of the Human Rights Commissioner that authorities needed to allow the protection of peaceful demonstrators and journalists covering these protests against violent individuals. Secret agencies in France have established a modern-professional operational mechanism amidst consecutive attacks of terrorist and radicalized forces. Though there is criticism in parliament and media reforms, overall and all-inclusively their fight for internal security is on the road to recovery and a cut above.

This book highlights different types of political and social transformations in France. No doubt, I received precarious threats in case of written letters and telephone calls, but I never relinquished my academic and intellectual struggle against the sarcastic forces. I was harassed repeatedly, and harmed. The legal framework for the French intelligence received less attention from Parliamentarians and successive governments, but surveillance measures were in place to help the police in managing law and order. The French domestic and external intelligence agencies have often received harsh criticism in social media for some of their underwhelming acts. Adopted by the Parliament in June 2015, the President corroborated the new surveillance law on July 24, 2015 and published it in an Official Journal in July 2015. In my articles and research papers published in newspapers and journals in 2015, I have already suggested some intelligence reforms in France to break the ring of terrorist and jihadist organizations. The 2015 terrorist attacks in Paris exhibited police failure in France. The French government later constituted a fusion of all intelligence agencies to effectively respond to the threat of radicalization and international terrorism. After intelligence and security sector reforms, terrorist incidents decreased in France. After these reforms, the threat of terrorism decreased but the threat of foreign spying has exponentially exacerbated.

The Yellow Vest and the recent civil disobedience and terrorist, in which terrorist groups of all EU member states, illegal extremist and terrorist, Pakistani, Afghan and African looters demonstrated their power in France's cities and towns and that was a golden opportunity they established their networks on improvised bases. From 2015 to 2023, after terrorist attacks in France, several law enforcement and intelligence reforms have been introduced in the country to manage internal security and foreign espionage professionally, but lack of public confidence and lack of coordination are still discussed in intellectual forums and newspapers. An intelligence failure can be analysed in two different ways. The first is to differentiate between strategic and operational warning. The second is to examine the different components of the intelligence process to evaluate whether there were missed opportunities. The 2015 security sector reform and formation of a fusion helped law enforcement agencies to effectively counter terrorism and radicalization. In Eastern European states, the former Communist culture of intelligence is yet so strongly rooted in society and resists all new efforts of bringing intelligence under democratic control. In Greece, Lithuania, Estonia, Ukraine, Romania, and Poland, private, political, and bureaucratic stakeholders have generated numerous problems. By law, all EU member states need to regulate organizations of their country's intelligence services and establish different units to divide responsibilities between military and civilian agencies.

Musa Khan Jalalzai
London

# Chapter 1

# National Security Threat Perceptions and Countering Foreign Espionage Strategies: The EU and the French Security Reform

After the tail-end of the cold war, the EU member states never realised seriousness of emerging national security threats, radicalization and extremism that ruined dozens of states in Asia and Africa and are still dancing in towns and streets. These organizations and their leadership, who played for different states in military conflicts, proxy wars and political destabilization, now reached Europe and established their terror networks there. The European Union member states should have taken intelligence and security sector reforms seriously to fit their forces to fight against these evil forces and democratize their agencies and forces under the principles of their constitutions. They needed to relinquish the first and second world wars rotten intelligence and policing infrastructures and introduce reforms in order to bring all these forces under modern democratic control. However,[1] have thoroughly and from top to bottom studied major European intelligence and policing agencies and their old operational mechanism and put in writing more than ten books on this issue. In my books (published), I drew attention to the need for security sectors and intelligence reforms to better manage domestic governance and external threats amidst the exponentially growing and strengthening body of extremism and international terrorism.

In yesteryears, my preceding and precursory work on intelligence analysis, operations and international cooperation received different pieces of information, cannonball and notices, which inculcated me to paint a different picture of security and law enforcement mechanisms in Europe. This book highlights different types of political and social transformations in the EU. No doubt I received precarious threats in case of written letters and telephone calls, but I never relinquished my academic and intellectual struggle against the sarcastic forces. Newspapers and journal articles noted globalization and the transformation of the fear market facilitated the noteworthiness of the works of secret agencies in all EU member states. The post-cold war era prompted the introduction of modern security sector reforms and strategies. The fear market across Europe has become a profitable business that results from the complex nature of the security threat and the cost of countering the threat of radicalization and extremism.

The EU has been experiencing a revival of right and left-wing extremism and radicalization. All but ten years ago, the EU was awarded for its sixty years living in peace and democracy. After the Russian invasion of Ukraine, the United States started pushing Europe to relinquish importing Russian oil and gas, and planned to deindustrialize Europe, control its market by introducing so-called liberal policies. The US army destroyed the German industry by blowing off the North-Stream gas pipeline. Now the European Union is facing serious economic and political challenges on all fronts. No doubt, the EU has developed internal markets, and energy regulation, but its hands have been tied with the US strand. The United States has long been attempting to mould other countries and the world order with its values and political system to promote democracy and human rights. The EU is now facing hybrid threats and violent extremism. Intelligence cooperation among the EU states failed to cultivate a strong relationship with policy makers and stakeholders. (The underlying causes of strategic surprise in EU foreign policy: a post-mortem investigation of the Arab uprisings and the Ukraine–Russia crisis of 2013/14. Nikki Ikani and Christoph O.Meyer, European security-2022).[1]

Over the past 20 years, EU intelligence infrastructures lived through numerous management crises and ordeals. The dismemberment of the Union of the Soviet gave birth to more states in Eastern Europe. These states have been struggling to introduce security sector reform and bring a new form of intelligence under democratic control since 2001. They failed because the former Soviet era intelligence infrastructure is so strong and resists their reforms strategies. Consequently, they are still fighting for Europeanization of that intelligence infrastructure. Romania, Poland, Latvia, Estonia, parts of Germany, Norway and even Brussels failed to establish a strong intelligence infrastructure under democratic control. If we look at the present cooperation mechanism between EU states, we can judge from the fact that intelligence interoperability and cooperation has failed to foster a strong and encouraging relationship with policy makers.

Former Prime Minister Boris Johnson's extra-nationalistic and jingoistic approach to modern diplomacy vanished all hopes of a good and friendly relationship with Europe. The tension between the two side conflagration over the border of Northern Ireland, and dynamics of the Johnson administration's domestic and foreign policy failed to address internal security crisis and international disinterestedness.[2] Privatization of intelligence, or dependency on private sector intelligence companies in Europe has become a topic of discussion of intellectual forums. The fact of the matter is that private surveillance and intelligence companies have never been effective in the case of law and order and national stability. They are working for money, not national interests, and partaking in conflict and civil wars-complication conflicts and policy making.

Dozens of states have been dependent on private policing and intelligence infrastructures due to the dearth of their manpower and professional security approach. In my previous books (Published): 1-Fixing the EU Intel Crisis: Intelligence Sharing, Law Enforcement and the Threat of Chemical Biological and Nuclear Terrorism. Algora Publishing, (New York-Aug. 2016); 2-The Intelligence War in Britain: Public Perceptions of the UK Intelligence Agencies, Foreign Espionage, the Tory Party and its Response to the Salisbury Attacks. (India-30 Nov. 2022); 3-Spying with Little Eye: Complexity of Intelligence Challenges in Europe, and the UK, Interference of Russian, Chinese and Iranian Intelligence, Oversight of Intelligence Infrastructure and Post Snow Reforms-2023; 4-The UK Big-3: The French and German Intelligence Reforms, Intelligence Diversity and Foreign Espionage; 5-The US Leaked Files, State Secrecy and Democratic Intelligence Oversight in Europe (30 Aug. 2023).

I have highlighted all the above mentioned security challenges and dearth of security sector reforms. Sharp criticism of the EU member states against each other points to an important question about the border security and immigration crisis in the region. The last few decades have experienced an increasing all-round and resourceful intelligence sharing on law enforcement level among the EU member states to make sure security, and fight against terrorism, but after the Russian invasion of Ukraine, they changed their perceptions.[3] (The UK Big-3: The French and German Intelligence Reforms, Intelligence Diversity and Foreign Espionage. Musa Khan Jalalzai-2022).

Author and expert, Martin, Alex in his paper has noted intelligence reforms in Eastern Europe where former communist security infrastructure was in place. He also highlighted security threats in this region and stressed the need for a functional intelligence architecture to fight against international terrorism, extremism and radicalization. He understands that western intelligence agencies have viewed intelligence services in reforming states as tactical opportunities and sources of intelligence rather than as targets for reform in the context of a wider reform agenda. In his view, 'practice of countering terrorism has altered the nature of intelligence gathering in ways that make accountability and public legitimacy more central to the effectiveness of intelligence services than the 'traditional' threats did'. Western models of intelligence oversight and accountability, according to Martin, Alex, are inadequate in states without developed traditions of democratic governance and weaknesses in wider political culture means that these models are not effective in lending intelligence services popular legitimacy." (The lessons of Eastern Europe for modern intelligence reform. Conflict, Security and Development, Volume 7, Number 4, December 2007)[4]

National Security threat perception and countering foreign espionage strategies in every member state was diversified while their response to international terrorism flattered underwhelming. Intelligence agencies in all EU member states were not sure of the reciprocation of their partners. Some states remarked their security was not under threat. Some intelligence agencies feared that their big partners might not share their national data on terrorism and radicalization. Mistrust and disinformation spread across Europe. In 2020, Boris Johnson's administration published a weak Russian intelligence report, while in 2022 and 2023, the British government yelled about the interference of Russian, Iranian and Chinese intelligence agencies. Experts and analysts, Pietro Castelli Gattinara and Caterina Froio in their analysis have documented tension between national and supranational sovereignty and the crisis of EU member states. They understand political conflict in Europe is no longer limited to restricted elite sectors, but now includes a broad range of collective actors in the electoral and protest arena. They view the changing scenario of recent far-right protests at the border between France and Italy as a newly emerging conflict.[5] (Politicizing Europe on the far right: Anti-EU mobilization across the party and non-party sector in France. Social Movement Studies-07 Jul 2021)

Domestic crises within members of the European Union in the last decade have raised serious doubts about the sustainability of a democratic Europe. Political and security sector reform have also prompted unrest and demonstration. France is still a strong democratic state that plays an important role in world politics. After the Russian war in Ukraine, all EU member states looked at their intelligence and counterintelligence capabilities as to whether they can counter Russian intelligence. Notwithstanding the Russian threat, the speed of intelligence reforms is slow while their involvement in the Ukraine war has also generated a trust deficit crisis. France is a strong Western European country that borders Spain to the south and Italy, Switzerland, Luxembourg, Belgium, and Germany to the east. France remains a major global power. Over the past decade, the European Union experienced a number of crises threatening its core policy regimes and the future of its polity. A series of protests began in France on 19 January 2023 with a demonstration of over one million people nationwide. President Emmanuel Macron reacted to the looming national security threat and the threat of terrorism in case of burning and looting in cities and towns.

Government surveillance measures are always undermined by fragmented oversight. Recent commentary of the Stiftung Neue Verantwortung has noted that 'if oversight bodies do not cooperate effectively with their European peers, compliance with basic human rights and data protection rules as well as the effectiveness of intelligence cooperation cannot be independently assessed'. The SNV also noted that European governments adopted new intelligence laws over the past few years since the Snowden revelations. But these reforms could not appease the widely held concerns about insufficient protections for human rights such as privacy and freedom of expression. (European Intelligence Oversight Network, the Stiftung Neue Verantwortung (SNV).[6]

The legal framework for the French intelligence received less attention from Parliamentarians and successive governments, but surveillance measures were in place to help the police in managing law and order. The French domestic and external intelligence agencies have been demonstrating professionally in Africa for decades, where their intelligence units helped the French army and local military forces in fighting international terrorism and sectarian wars. Adopted by the Parliament in June 2015, the President corroborated the new surveillance law on July 24, 2015, and published in an Official Journal in July 2015. There are many holes that facilitate foreign spy networks infiltration into French institutions and society.

These foreign intelligence units have been involved in recruiting local criminal and sectarian elements to force law enforcement agencies to deploy extra forces in streets. In July 2023, the French government authorized the police and law enforcement agencies to surreptitiously use mobile phones and other devices as their own surveillance tools in order to easily detect foreign funded organizations and sarcastic individuals.

France needed to document all residents and identify who is who living in cities and towns and where. Who is legal and who is illegal and what is their sectarian and religious background. Intelligence and the police need to extend their network to remote villages, towns and cities in order to bring all criminals and sectarian mafia groups into their book.[7] (The UK Big-3: The French and German Intelligence Reforms, Intelligence Diversity and Foreign Espionage. Musa Khan Jalalzai-2022).

The far right violence in France r-emerged with new strategies and new plans. Numerous articles and journal papers highlighted recent violence in France where foreign intelligence was making things worse. Notwithstanding the introduction of security sector and police reform, sectarian, extremists, foreign funded organizations and jihadist mafia groups have been a greater challenge since 2001. The Euronews on 09 July 2023 reported France's intelligence authorities of violent actions by the ultra-right organizations. Director General of France Domestic Intelligence, Nicholas Lerner in his interview with Le Monde newspaper warned that "we have witnessed very worrying resurgence of violent action".[8] He also warned in his interview that senior civil servants were concerned. He also said, "The fight against global warming is a legitimate battle that deserves to be fought with determination. The French far right in the political sphere has painted several faces. The General Directorate for Internal Security is a French Security Agency. It is charged with counter-espionage, counter-terrorism, countering cybercrime and surveillance of potentially threatening groups, organisations, and social phenomena. The agency was created in 2008 under the name Central Directorate of Interior Intelligence. The French successive governments have introduced intelligence and security sector reforms to make intelligence competent.

According to the French Foreign Minister Catherine Colonna remarks that 'Russian actors had been involved in a digital information manipulation campaign, including several in Europe. German Interior Minister Nancy Faeser's report confirmed the involvement of Chinese intelligence that has focused on protecting the country's national interests in Europe. "To maintain control over the Chinese diaspora, overseas police stations are run by "Chinese expatriates loyal to the line–often with German citizenship." Alina Clasen noted. State transformation and security sector reforms in Germany have further professionalized tactics of domestic and foreign intelligence agencies. In 2022, foreign espionage, radicalization and extremism have taken root there, while Chinese, Iranian, Turkish and Russian secret agencies have been operating in all European states. Expert and analyst Alina Clasen in her recent analysis (Intelligence reform and the transformation of the state: the end of a French exception German intelligence services point to increased hybrid security threats. EURACTIV. de-19 July 2023) has quoted the German domestic intelligence services (BfV) and German Minister of the Interior Nancy Faeser reports on the intelligence reforms and interference of foreign agencies in domestic affairs of Germany and other EU member states:

"Espionage, illegitimate influence peddling, disinformation campaigns, and cyber-attacks increased in Germany in 2022, with activities mainly linked to Russia, China, Iran, and Turkey, according to a report by the domestic intelligence services (BfV) published on Tuesday (20 June). The Federal Office for the Protection of the Constitution sees a connection between the increase in hybrid threats and the Russian war of aggression against Ukraine initiated in February 2022 and China's growing confrontational approach with the West. "The criminal Russian war of aggression against Ukraine has changed the security situation across Europe. We have taken strong measures to arm ourselves against espionage, disinformation campaigns, and cyberattacks," explained German Minister of the Interior Nancy Faeser at the presentation of the report on Tuesday (20 June). Besides Russia, the main actors are China, Iran, and Turkey, and the impact of activities–like cyberattacks, disinformation, and espionage – varies. The report emphasises that the illegal actions of foreign intelligence services affect national sovereignty and cause considerable operational and economic damage. In particular, the increased use of social media as a means for disinformation was identified with the aim of weakening social cohesion, disrupting the free formation of opinion, and destabilising democracy."[9]

French intelligence was implicated in a multifaceted crisis, while if we look at its past historical status, French intelligence has been a competent agency during the First and Second World Wars, and extensive Cold War. In his Al Jazeera analysis, Bruce Crumley noted that the Paris attacks occurred due to the police failure. He has also documented the US warning about the ISIS attacks in France. He is of the opinion that terrorists were on the radar of French authorities as radicals and potential threats—with at least one charged in a terrorism-related case. (Were the Paris attacks a French intelligence failure? Al Jazeera November 17, 2015).[10] On 23 December 2022, BBC reported a gunman opened fire in central Paris, killing three people and wounding three others. The attacker targeted a Kurdish cultural centre and shot local community members. The police investigated a possible racist motive.[11] On 28 October 2020, Paris based Le Monde reported the killing of three people in a knife attack at a church in Nice, in what French President Emmanuel Macron said was an "Islamist terrorist attack". He said France would not surrender its core values after visiting the Notre-Dame basilica in the southern city. An extra 4,000 troops are being deployed to protect churches and schools.

Moreover, on 05 July 2016, Associated Press reported multiple failings by French policing agencies including their lack of cooperation with agencies, communities and political leadership.[12] "Our police have failed," Fenech said at a news conference called to present proposals growing out of the nearly six-month investigation....Investigators found that intelligence was not the only failure rivalry and rules stymied various police and military units who arrived at the scene of the November Paris attacks.[13] The French inquiry argued changes to intelligence services in light of failures. An investigative committee of France's Parliament announced that it had found intelligence lapses leading up to the November terror attacks in Paris. Georges Fenech, head of the special parliamentary commission noted the Paris 2015 attacks: "Our intelligence services have failed. On 05 July 2016, New York Times (Aurelien Breeden) reported a parliamentary committee examining two devastating terrorist attacks in France in 2015, "called for the nation's intelligence agencies to be streamlined and merged, finding widespread failures in the collection and analysis of information that could have helped prevent the attacks.[14]

Once again France's intelligence agencies confronted extremist and radicalized elements in streets and towns to intercept them from looting, and destroying shops, historical places and markets in 2023. The French government focussed on intelligence and security sector reforms, while never taking social reforms seriously in order to integrate all extremists, radicalised jihadists and sarcastic so-called Muslims into the French society. More than sixty years after the promulgation of the first intelligence act, French lawmakers once more want some intelligence and security sector reforms. Expert and journalist, Jacques Follorou in his commentary on the French intelligence reforms (France's tepid intelligence reform, 07 June 2021, About Intel) is of the view that by these reforms "government also aims to provide new capabilities to the services. The bill includes a provision dedicated to the surveillance of a new generation of satellites. Small in size, placed by the thousands in low orbit, these satellites provide high-speed Internet access outside of traditional operators, and escape the "big ears" of intelligence. The government wants to fill this gap, just as it wants to legislate a way to bypass the technical hurdles posed by 5G networks. Since 2016, a terrorism-related data storage centre, nicknamed "the warehouse", has been operating outside any legal framework. Article L. 863-2 of the Internal Security Code, also adopted in 2016, provides that intelligence agencies can "share all the information useful for the accomplishment of their missions".[15]

In my articles and research papers published in newspapers and journals in 2015, I have already suggested some intelligence reforms in France to break the ring of terrorist and jihadist organizations. The 2015 terrorist attacks in Paris exhibited police failure in France. The French government, later on, constituted a fusion of all intelligence agencies to effectively respond to the threat of radicalization and international terrorism. After intelligence and security sector reforms, terrorist incidents decreased in France. Writers and experts, Griff Witte and Loveday Morris (Failure to stop Paris attacks reveals fatal flaws at heart of European security-Washington Post, 28 November 2015) also noted in their analysis terrorist attacks that left 130 people dead in Paris, the killers relied on a cunning awareness of the weaknesses at the heart of the European security services charged with stopping them: "Poor information-sharing among intelligence agencies, a threadbare system for tracking suspects across open borders and an unmanageably long list of home-grown extremists to monitor all gave the Paris plotters an opening to carry out the deadliest attack on French soil in more than half a century. Two weeks later, European security experts say the flaws in the continent's defenses are as conspicuous as ever, with no clear plan for fixing them. "We lack the most obvious tools to deal with this threat," said Jean-Charles Brisard, chairman of the Paris-based Centre for the Analysis of Terrorism.[16]

France has entered a political, social and economic transformation phase. The Niger crisis and military takeover has deeply disturbed political and military leadership of the country, and the arrival of Wagner militia and other stakeholders created a threatening security environment. In all these and other events, French intelligence exhibited its professional approach and proved that a strong and reformed secret agency can better manage national security crises. In fact secret agencies were not conceived in France as a functional tool in the hands of the decision-maker, but later on they realized the importance of intelligence infrastructure. Persistent intelligence and security sector reforms were in fact the reorganization and reinvention of French security infrastructure. As France has been a strong colonial power, its agencies have also been struggling to adopt modern intelligence tactics. French reform is based on the action of an attempt to explain or justify behaviour or an attitude of secret agencies with logical reasons, or mechanism in which apparent logical reasons are given to justify behaviour. Government and the state have decided to modernise and centralise secret agencies. Expert and writer, Anne Lise Michelot (Reform of the French Intelligence Oversight System-30 November 2028) has documented some aspects of the French intelligence oversight and reform:

"French intelligence remains a very secretive world from the public view, and the little presence it occupies in the press or public debate is more often than not one of scandal, abuse or failure. In 2008, the government initiated a reform process of the intelligence organisation, and continued in 2015, following the numerous terrorist attacks on the national territory. The result of this long process of reshaping the intelligence community has included attempts at perfecting, and in some cases creating, oversight mechanisms. These reforms have been the subject of public and parliamentary debates for the past decade, as many politicians, scholars and journalists pointed out the lack of supervision and the relative freedom intelligence agencies enjoyed in performing their activities. Today, the French oversight system comprises a specific institution for each type of control. This diversified/plural system was completed with the creation of a new institution, the Commission Nationale de Contrôle des Techniques de Renseignement, CNCTR (national commission for the control of intelligence techniques) in 2015. The creation of the CNCTR in 2015 to oversee the usage of intelligence techniques has attempted to bring France up to high democratic standards in terms of intelligence oversight. However, the commission's limited means hinder its ability to perform fully its duties."[17]

After these reforms, the threat of terrorism decreased but the threat of foreign spying has exponentially exacerbated. Foreign spies attempted on many occasions to create civil unrest and infiltrate their spies into the system of the country. The Yellow Vest and the recent civil disobedience and terrorists looting and burning campaign, in which terrorist groups of all EU member states, illegal extremist and terrorist, Pakistani, Afghan and African looters demonstrated their power in France's cities and towns, and that was a golden opportunity they established their networks on improvised bases. They transported their spies and intelligence units-adorned with military grade weapons to the cities and towns of France. In an interview with Le Monde newspaper, the head (Nicolas Lerner has been director general of the Directorate General of Internal Security

(DGSI), France›s domestic intelligence agency) of the country's domestic intelligence agency described the country›s potential security threats.

The French political environment is currently undergoing structural changes spearheaded by the Presidency. France has previously suffered major terrorist attacks and remained a prominent target for extremist and radicalized groups. Major businesses and financial firms have managed their own security privately as the country faces an elevated terrorist threat. From 2015 to 2023, after terrorist attacks in France, several law enforcement and intelligence reforms have been introduced in the country to manage internal security and foreign espionage professionally, but lack of public confidence and lack of coordination are still discussed in intellectual forums and newspapers. The 2015 security sector reform and formation of a fusion helped law enforcement agencies to effectively counter terrorism and radicalization. In 2021, and 2023, more changes were added to the infrastructure of law enforcement and intelligence. Expert and journalist, Jacques Follorou (France's tepid intelligence reform-07 June, 2021) in his paper documented new developments of policing and intelligence reform in France:

"The government wants to fill this gap, just as it wants to legislate a way to bypass the technical hurdles posed by 5G networks. Although, on paper, the bill seems to bring only a limited number of changes, the French government is definitely taking intelligence into the age of Artificial Intelligence (AI). It aims to authorise the use of mass collection of private communications data for the research and development of new surveillance tools based on machine learning. To become operational, AI needs to digest vast troves of real personal data. The proposed bill therefore distinguishes a "training phase," during which overpowered algorithms will grind our data just to train AI models, and an "operational phase," where personal data will, this time, be subject to the legal framework. To mitigate the risks of abuse, the text subjects this system to the oversight of the National Commission for the Control of Intelligence Techniques (CNCTR), an advisory but independent body, which issues an opinion on all government surveillance. Article L. 863-2 of the Internal Security Code, also adopted in 2016, provides that intelligence agencies can "share all the information useful for the accomplishment of their missions".[18]

Chapter 2

# The French Intelligence Reform, Jihadist Groups and the Threat of Radicalization, Nuclear and Biological Terrorism

On 13 November 2015, a series of terrorist attacks trembled the French law enforcement infrastructure that killed more than 130 innocent people and many other injured. Concerns were raised that Paris-based radicalized elements may take arms to challenge authority of the state and government. Intelligence and law enforcement agencies struggled to prevent action of foreign stakeholders, fought terrorism and radicalization professionally, and introduced extensive surveillance mechanisms. The fusion was formed on the demand of Interior Minister Nicolas Sarkozy. Fusion was a good idea but as the wave of terrorism exacerbated, its performance became strong as well. France's relationship with the Muslim world and its own radicalized elements has been deeply complex. French Muslim are not so educated and civilised people due to their culture of conservatism. Experts and analysts, John Wihbey and Leighton Walter Kille in their commentary (France, Islam, terrorism and the challenges of integration: Research roundup, The Journalist's Resources. November 16, 2015), have noted some aspects of the 2015 terrorist attacks in Paris:

"Examining the January 2015 incident may provide clues about the direction of French society in the wake of another attack. Immediately after the Charlie Hebdo killings there were hundreds of spontaneous mass demonstrations across Europe condemning the senseless violence, defending the liberty of the press and urging tolerance. A January 11 march calling for unity brought together over 1.3 million people, including more than 40 present and former heads of state. In May, France passed a wide-reaching surveillance law intended to improve the ability of the country's intelligence services to identify potential terrorists. While the law was strongly supported by the government, some condemned it as paving the way for mass surveillance on the order of that undertaken by the National

Security Agency (NSA) in the United States. In general, French society is more tolerant of religious mockery and satire than some other Western nations. Charlie Hebdo's fierce independence has long attracted admiration and criticism, as does its relentless pursuit of politicians and public figures who abused the public trust. Nothing was sacred, least of all religion: Child abuse by Catholic priests and violence by self-proclaimed protectors of Islam were both considered fair game. After a Danish newspaper published cartoons of the Prophet Muhammad in 2005, Charlie Hebdo printed them again to demonstrate the importance of the free press in an open society. Their offices were firebombed in 2011 after an issue that was supposedly "guest edited" by Muhammad, and had since regularly received threats of violence".[1]

On 05 July 2016, New York Times reported the French parliamentary committee examination of two terrorist attacks in 2015 that killed innocent people and badly affected national critical infrastructure. The committee said that all intelligence agencies needed to be fixed due to their underwhelming demonstrations in the past. In more than 40 proposals, parliamentarians urged that the government needed to merge intelligence agencies, or make a fusion in order to establish a national agency to fight the looming threat of terrorism and radicalization. The lower house of Parliament also formed a committee to investigate attacks on the newspapers office of Charlie Hebdo in Paris. Committee allowed France's largest parties including socialist party to partake in that investigation.[2] Commentator and analyst, Aurelien Breeden (French Inquiry Urges Changes to Intelligence Services in Light of Failures-New York Times, 05 July, 2016) documented names of those terrorists who ruined lives of French citizens:

"The Nov. 13 attacks were largely organized by a cell of Islamic State militants operating from Brussels. The team also carried out attacks in and around the Belgian capital on March 22 that left 32 people dead and hundreds of others injured. As many as six of the assailants in the coordinated Islamic State terrorist assault in Paris were Europeans who had traveled to Syria. Many of the attackers in that cell were known to the French or Belgian authorities; some had even been under surveillance. "Clearly, Europe is not up to the task in the fight against terrorism, even if progress has been made in the past months," said Sébastien Pietrasanta, the top Socialist lawmaker on the committee....The committee urged European Union member states to give Europol, the bloc's law enforcement agency, and Frontex, the bloc's border-control agency, full access to the Schengen Information System, a database of missing or wanted people.[3] The New York Times reported Salah Abdeslam, the only direct participant in the November attacks was arrested in Belgium in March and extradited to France in April, but he refused to answer questions. He was suspected of playing an important role in the logistical planning of the plot, but his role on the night of the attacks was less clear. Mr. Abdeslam, a French citizen of Moroccan ancestry who lived in Belgium, eluded capture for four months after the attacks".[4]

The Paris attacks ruined the lives of 130 people, in which professionals and students were also targeted. The French intelligence agencies have long been secretive from the public, which resulted in their lack of public confidence. In 2008, the government initiated a reform process of the intelligence organisation that continued up until 2021. These reforms were initiated after debates in Parliament, several intellectuals and politicians raised the question of public confidence and oversight mechanisms. Later on, a body of CNCTR was formed to watch the work of agencies as an independent commission. The CNCTR makes a non-binding recommendation to the Prime Minister, who is in charge of the approval. Reviews can also be carried out after implementation of the technique, in particular, to ensure that it is not continued without justified motives. Analyst and expert, Anne Lise Michelot (Reform of the French Intelligence Oversight System, the Security Distillery- November 30, 2018) has highlighted performance and achievement of the CNCTR commission: "The creation of the CNCTR in 2015 to oversee the usage of intelligence techniques has attempted to bring France up to high democratic standards in terms of intelligence oversight. However, the commission's limited means hinder its ability to perform its duties fully. And let's not forget that its recommendations are not binding! These considerations require particular attention now that France has entered the age of mass data collection, with the first IMSI-catchers set up in November 2017 and no additional workforce for the CNCTR in sight. There is still some way to go before fully democratic intelligence oversight is achieved."[5]

After the 2015 terrorist attacks in France, the country was maintaining six intelligence agencies and some other services, which contributed to the collection of intelligence. Analyst and expert, Eric Denece (French Intelligence and Security Services in 2016, a Short History. Note, Historique No 47, December 2016. Centre Français de Recherche sur le Renseignement (CF2R) in its paper noted six intelligence agencies of France in 2016 but I want to mention here only four agencies. The General Directorate of external security, the strong and largest agency. Defence intelligence and security Directorate, General Directorate for Internal Security and National Directorate for Customs Intelligence. Among these agencies, The DGSE, DRM and DPSD are attached to the Ministry of Defence, the DGSI is attached to the Ministry of the Interior and the DNRED and TRACFIN are attached to the Ministry of Economy and Finance.[6] The issue of oversight has received bundles of appreciation and criticism keeping in view the current law and order management crisis. Oversight received criticism in newspapers as extremist and radicalized forces challenged authority of law enforcement in Paris. Expert of intelligence studies, Félix Tréguer in his research paper (Intelligence Reform and the Snowden Paradox: The Case of France) noted some legal development in France:

"Over the course of the parliamentary debate, and in particular when the Senate adopted amendments to the Bill in first reading in October 2013, the law became the vehicle for a partial legalisation of the new capabilities. We were just four months after the first Snowden disclosures, and again no human rights organisation reacted. Six weeks later however, an industry group representing online social services including Google France, AOL, eBay, Facebook, Microsoft, Skype and French companies like Deezer or Dailymotion published an article against the reform (Association des Services Internet Communautaires, 2013). It was only then that human rights groups understood the importance of this provision and mounted a last-minute effort to get the provision out of the bill. Coming at a very late stage of the legislative procedure, the effort eventually failed to strike out the provision … .In July 2014, just as the government was introducing a new anti-terrorism bill before the Parliament, President François Hollande convened a National Intelligence Council at the Élysée Palace. In the laconic press-release issued on that day, the Council claimed to have "determined the strategic priorities of [intelligence] services and approved the legal, technical and human resources necessary to carry on these priorities" (French Presidency, 2014). The debate on the anti-terrorism bill, finally adopted in November 2014, also gave an opportunity to OLN members to engage in their first coordinated action against the law's new restrictions on freedom of expression online. But on January 25th 2015, then Prime Minister Manuel Valls turned the long-awaited intelligence reform into an essential part of the government's political response to the Paris attacks carried on earlier that month."[7]

Counterterrorism approach and mechanism has been facing hindrances in Europe since the 7/7 terrorist attacks in London and the 2015 attacks in Paris. There are countless research papers and articles that highlight the failure of EU agencies to control radicalized forces. Expert and analyst, Alex Mackenzie (Conspicuous by their absence? The member states in the European Union counter-terrorism. Journal of European Integration-11 September 2023) in his paper documented efforts of counterterrorism agencies. The 2015 Charlie Hebdo attacks prompted the seriousness of domestic security in France: "The terrorist attacks in Paris in November 2015 by returnee foreign fighters killed over 100 people and injured hundreds more....The French government is considered to have 'spearheaded the drive' for EU-PNR from here (EurActiv 2016) and used a range of entrepreneurial techniques against opposition MEPs: lobbying, warning of serious consequences, and chiding them for irresponsibility."[8]

Experts and policy makers raised the question of intelligence failure, but that was not failure of intel it was failure of police and the lack of coordination between law enforcement agencies. Analyst Timothy Holman (14 December 2015) has divided intelligence failure in two ways; differentiation between strategic and operational warning and examination of different components of intelligence process.[9] This is his own perception but there are several other elements that cause intelligence failure in war and peace time such as the lack of adequate intelligence information, lack of trained manpower, failure to understand modern technology, lack of proper intelligence sharing with policymakers, and lack of actionable intelligence. In the aftermath of the terrorist attacks in London, Manchester, Paris and Germany, the EU intelligence agencies became subject to hot-blooded assessment.

Notwithstanding the introduction of the Mass Surveillance System and monitoring programme that deeply collect sensitive information about foreign espionage, foreign intelligence agencies in the EU maintain strong espionage networks. Why do the EU secret intelligence agencies fail repeatedly? Is it because of the lack of adequate intelligence, the dearth of trained manpower in the intelligence sector, failure to apply latest sophisticated technology in surveillance, lack of proper, intelligence sharing between the Centre and the states, lack of action on available intelligence, or the lack of sensible intelligence reforms? There are reports that Russian and Chinese intelligence agencies have established spy networks in some EU member states to closely monitor internal social and political crises. Expert, Timothy Holman (Paris: An Intelligence Failure or a Failure to Understand the Limits of Intelligence? 14 December 2015. RUSI) has raised important question domestic security including the threat of extremism in France:

"At the strategic level, the French intelligence (DGSE) and security (DGSI) agencies had identified the threat to France from Daesh, Jabhat Al-Nusra (JaN), Al-Qaeda-affiliated entities active in Yemen and the Sahel, as well as France-based sympathisers of these groups. The strategic environment had been mapped and this can be seen in the efforts to acquire extra resources through financial means as well as increased collection permissions through changes to legislation. Speaking recently in the US, the director of the DGSE was very clear about the nature of the threat facing France. At the operational level, authorities are dealing with groups and individuals suspected of planning an attack or of having the capacity to do so. This level is more complex than the strategic level as it requires the identification of particular individuals or groups of individuals involved in specific plotting. The intelligence process is the same: identification, collection, analysis and mitigation. The four areas are complex enough when the target set is limited but even more so when there are potentially thousands of individuals and multiple threat streams – groups in Yemen, Iraq and Syria, Mali, Somalia, and then individuals acting alone or relatively spontaneously".[10]

Writers and experts in their research papers and articles highlighted in detail the 2015 Paris terrorist attacks, and placed the blame on France's internal security intelligence that the police and intelligence had failed to intercept terrorists entering the city. This author also highlighted this issue in articles and papers with different perspectives. In Asian and African papers and newspaper stories, the French intelligence was held accountable for the failure to act on time, but in major newspapers in France and some European academic circles the police were held accountable not the intelligence agencies. Personally, I think intelligence failure has some grounds and causes behind terrorist incidents. Expert Janani Krishnaswamy in her research thesis (Policy Report No-3, Why Intelligence Fails, the Hindu Centre for Politics and Public Policy-2013) has noted some grounds of intelligence failure in a country that faces national security challenges. She views sources of intelligence failure not only within the boundaries of secret spy agencies but understands that in the 'inaction of policy makers to react on the intelligence made available, the intelligence community's inability to adapt to the changing faces of terror, and the reform maker's failure to make appropriate proposals of intelligence reforms'. During the catastrophe and law and order mismanagement crisis intelligence information collectors are indicted for failure, but she is on the view that the story of intelligence is far from complete:

"Even if some reforms were sensible in fixing a few troubles of the intelligence community, reform makers have not been able to mend the core predicaments of the community because of (a) a failure to make any post-event audits, (b) lack of professionalism and systematised functioning, (c) communication gap between producers and consumers of intelligence and lack of protocol for engaging and de-engaging, (d) failure to implement reforms to recruit and train intelligent personnel, (e) failure to improve the working of intelligence personnel and (f) failure to adequately strengthen local intelligence. In the pages that follow, I will discuss each of these failures independently, and consequently expose the dangers of constricted reform making".[11] In his article, expert Timothy Holman (Paris: An Intelligence Failure or a Failure to Understand the Limits of Intelligence? Royal United Services Institute, London-14 December 2015) has noted some aspects of intelligence failure in France and viewed the failure of French intelligence during the terrorist attacks in Paris as miss-opportunities to prevent these attacks. In his analysis, writer Timothy Holman indicated that these terrorist attacks were carried out by jihadist groups based in Europe:

"All terrorist attacks, whether partially or completely successful, represent a failure of the state agencies charged with protecting the citizens of that state. But this does not necessarily equate to an intelligence failure, which implies that the intelligence process, or parts of it, did not function. An intelligence failure can be analysed in two different ways. The first is to differentiate between strategic and operational warning. The second is to examine the different components of the intelligence process to evaluate whether there were missed opportunities. At the strategic level, the French intelligence (DGSE) and security (DGSI) agencies had identified the threat to France from Daesh, Jabhat Al-Nusra (JaN), Al-Qaeda-affiliated entities active in Yemen and the Sahel, as well as France-based sympathisers of these groups. The strategic environment had been mapped and this can be seen in the efforts to acquire extra resources through financial means as well as increased collection permissions through changes to legislation. Speaking recently in the US, the director of the DGSE was very clear about the nature of the threat facing France".[12] The French General Directorate of foreign intelligence collection and operations is DGSE (Direction générale de la Sécurité extérieure) that protects the country's security through intelligence gathering and conducting paramilitary and counterintelligence operations abroad. The DGSE operates under the direction of the French Ministry of Armed Forces and works alongside its domestic counterpart, the DGSI (General Directorate for Internal Security).

Janani Krishnaswamy in her research thesis (Policy Report No-3, Why Intelligence Fails, the Hindu Centre for Politics and Public Policy-2013) also views the Failures of intelligence is associated with a failure of the intelligence community to adapt itself based on the changing needs of the community, there are different perception of the causes of intelligence failures in a democratic state: No doubt, Parliamentary and legal oversight is the best source to provide appropriate mechanisms for intelligence. 'However, given the complexity of creating such oversight mechanisms in the near future, here's what I think the producers and consumers of intelligence should consider doing to help intelligence scholars come up with solutions to avert the failures of the intelligence community in future'.[13] If we look at the recent turmoil of Niger coup, we can judge the conflict of opinion between the French President and its intelligence agencies as he placed blame on his spy agency for the failure over the Niger crisis. The blame game of intelligence failure in France was once more reported in newspapers and electronic media that the Niger government collapsed due to the failure of intelligence. The French President may have received contradictory information, as generally with limited powers, no agency can prevent a political and military crisis in a foreign country.

Arab News in its news report (French spy row as Macron accuses intelligence chief of failure over Niger coup, 03 August 2023), noted criticism of President Macron of his intelligence agencies over a perceived failure to predict the coup in Niger. France has been in control of the country since 1960. The President noted that the Director General for External Security, should have foreseen the coup, which would have allowed France to prevent the deposition of President Mohamed Bazoum. Arab News reported.[14] On 27 April 2023, John Leicester (Intelligence chief: Russian spy ring had 'source' in France) noted sworn testimony of the French intelligence Chief, in which Mr. Lerner remarked that Russia had long been running the largest spy operation in France, using intelligence officers posing as diplomats. In each Western country, several dozen officers—their number has diminished significantly since the start of the Ukraine crisis—from the three Russian intelligence services carrying out intelligence and interference actions under diplomatic cover." AP News noted.[15] This is a successful aspect of French intelligence that countered a foreign intelligence agency. However, Intelligence Chief Lerner warned parliamentarians to be vigilant about their security. Counterintelligence Chief Nicolas Lerner, was speaking to a French parliamentary enquiry looking into foreign efforts to influence or corrupt political parties. AP news noted.[16]

In France, the focus of Jihadist groups has been radicalization of the young generation since 2001, but it is unclear how many foreign fighters have ultimately claimed asylum in France, and under what objectives. Before the rise of ISIS, African and South Asian jihadist groups were operating in France to expand their terrorist networks. South Asian fighters linked to ISIS in Paris also participated in acts of terrorism in other countries. ISIS has previously restrained itself from getting involved in attacks in Europe, but after it trained EU citizens, the group entered into confrontations with the EU agencies. The rising intelligence presence of China and Russia in Europe, and the turbulence in Ukraine, Pakistan, and North Africa, all underscore the urgent need for a highly professional intelligence agency within the European Union. Religious cleric, Mufti Abdul Aziz of Lal Masjid Islamabad Pakistan, in his recent interview with a local journalist communicated that the Quran allows Muslims to become terrorists against the enemies of Allah, or infidels (Jews, Christians, and Hindu). His knowledge about the Holy Quran and Allah Almighty is shameful and deplorable. He generated controversies about Allah Almighty and the Holy Quran and remarked sacrilegiously about Allah.[17]

Pakistani Mullahs needed to reject his wrong interpretation of the Holy Quran, but never responded to his rumbling. The Holy Quran never ordered or directed Muslims to become terrorists against the enemy of Allah (Christians, Jews, Hindus, Sikhs, Paris, and Buddhists).[18] The concept of suicide attacks, or dying in order to kill in the name of religion becomes supreme ideal of Taliban and Pakistani Mullahs. After the US invasion of Afghanistan, Taliban resorted to suicide terrorism to force the United States and its NATO allies to withdraw their forces from the country, and restore Emirate Islami. Taliban and the IS-K became dominant forces in suicide terrorism to internationalise and justify it. Modern suicide terrorism emerged in Afghanistan after 9/11, but it was introduced in different shapes. Over the past two decades, the tactic of suicide terrorism in Afghanistan and Pakistan has been modified and justified by religious clerics. The fall of Afghanistan to the Taliban generated a new terror threat in Europe. The Taliban's close relationship with several EU terror groups and its inability to govern the whole country may turn Afghanistan into a nest of terror militias. In Afghanistan, close cooperation between Daesh and some disgruntled Taliban groups added to the pain of the Taliban Government.[19]

The establishment of Taliban's Suicide Brigades once more generated pain in the neck of Central Asia, Russia and Europe. Deployment of suchlike

Suicide Brigades next door to their borders of Central Asia are a major mainspring of consternation in the region. Europe refused to recognise the Taliban government and forewarned deployment of over 6,000 fighters of Suicide Brigade. Recent violence in Kazakhstan has proved my prognostication that terrorist and extremist organizations based in Europe can target civilian and military installations. Nuclear terrorism remains a constant threat to peace in Europe. A new addition to the list of terrorist organizations is Tablighi Jamaat of Pakistan that has established strong extremist networks in EU, Pakistan, India and Bangladesh. The Tablighi extremist units recently exhibited their power and professional capabilities by organising sarcastic elements against Kazakhstan's government in January 2022. Recent events in Kazakhstan and Tajikistan have raised the prospect of extremist and jihadist groups using biological, radiological and chemical weapons against military installations and national critical infrastructure in both states.[20]

The Tablighi Jamaat is also facilitating extremism and terrorism in South Asia and Europe, and recruits Muslims and Christians to balloon out its infrastructure. Harkat-ul-Mujahideen, the Taliban and al Qaeda are being facilitated in Afghanistan and Pakistan by Tablighi Jamaat. Once a facilitator identifies such candidates, he often will segregate them from the main congregation in the mosque or community centre and put them into small prayer circles or study groups where they can be more easily exposed to jihadist ideology, Stratfor noted.[21] The 07 July 2005, London bombings were facilitated (Mohammed Siddique Khan and Shahzad Tanweer) by Tablighi Jamaat. "After Khan and Tanweer left the Tablighi mosque, they began attending the smaller Iqra Learning Center bookstore in Beeston, where they reportedly were exposed to frequent political discussions about places such as Iraq, Kashmir and Chechnya". Stratfor noted.[22] Members of Tablighi Jamaat are actively in contact with the local population, building mosques, preaching centres, intelligence recruitment centres and collecting millions in EU currency to further expand its extremist and terrorist operations to Africa and Middle East. This author is witness to many faces of the Tablighi intelligence networks by visiting their centres times and again. Radicalization always emerges in specific places, and these places significantly shape the way people engage or disengage with extremist activities.

French intelligence has focused predominantly on the threat of Islamist radicalisation and jihadism, even though violent extremism is not bound by a certain ideology and neither is radicalisation. The government submitted, in December 2020, a bill to the parliamentarians with the purpose of tackling radicalisation. South Asia Democratic Forum in its research paper (Policy Brief 10–Tablighi Jamaat and its role in Global Jihad. South Asia Democratic Forum-11 December 2020) has uncovered an investigation undertaken by EU intelligence agencies against the illegal activities of Tablighi Jamaat. The France's intelligence agency, (General Directorate of Internal Security) in its 2018 comprehensive report (state of the situation regarding the lodging of Islamic fundamentalism in France), noted Tablighi Jamaat as one of the four most active extremist organizations in France.[23] The General Directorate of Internal Security has been watching the group's activities in France's educational institutions, where it recruits and groom its students, the DGSI noted.[24] The DGSI also noted in its report that, "through to the strong cohesion among active Tablighi–reinforced through religious practises, teaching missions, and omnipresent prayers among others–the social ties of adherents outside the Tablighi community disappear quickly the report warned.[25]

European intelligence agencies have established several surveillance units to closely watch terrorist and secret business of Tablighi Jamaat in towns and cities. Italian and Brussels intelligence agencies have become vigilant to prevent radicalized and extremist activities of Tablighi Jamaat, while German intelligence (BND) is cooperating with other EU members and experts of the European intelligence community to adopt professional measures in controlling the illegal activities of Tablighi Jamaat. The Tablighi intelligence units are bound to trace addresses of government officials, intelligence workers and its sectarian opponents across Europe. Having reviewed the prevailing threatening situation and illegal activities of Tablighi Jamaat in the Netherlands, General Intelligence and Security Service of the country (AVID) has also identified a new phase of radicalization in the country. Tablighi Jamaat has also established an extremist and intelligence network in the Netherlands where its workers have spread in towns and cities. The AVID stressed that Tablighi was a variant of radical Islam and 'manifest themselves in non-violent, radical-Islamic puritan groups'. In its report, South Asia Democratic Forum (Policy Brief 10–Tablighi Jamaat and its role in Global Jihad. South Asia Democratic Forum 11 December 2020) has reviewed concerns of Portugal intelligence agencies: "Serviço de Informações de Segurança" (SIS, Intelligence and Security Service).[26]

According to Maria do Céu Pinto, since 2001, the country's intelligence and law enforcing agencies have identified links 'between individuals residing in Portugal and radical Islamic operatives within the ideological network of Al Qaeda, as well as logistical and support activities for terrorism, namely of a criminal nature".[27] This is an interesting, excruciating and gut-wrenching story of Tablighi Jamaat that preaches and delivers sermons across Europe, but secretly operates as an intelligence agency. The group has been recently banned in some states, while it has changed its intelligence operational mechanism to dance with new tangos in Europe. The Tablighi Jamaat has been spying on some states for decades, collecting intelligence information from remote areas, terrorist nests, insurgent's centres and EU states. The group traces addresses for wanted political workers and critics across EU and South Asia, and brings more young and educated people into its clandestine networks. Former intelligence experts, military generals and militant organizations are the main target of the Tablighi intelligence infrastructure. Terrorist organisations suchlike ISIS, and the Taliban through Facebook, YouTube and twitter invite young people to join their networks by using various marketing techniques. These terror groups are marketers as well as consumers to a degree; their recruiters 'market' boys and use them as human bombs against civil society and military infrastructure. They supply suicide bombers across Asia and the Middle East very cheap. Religious and political vendettas are being settled by using suicide bombers against rival groups or families. This generation of fear and panic is controlled by extremist elements and non-state actors.

Pakistan's Tablighi Jamaat has established different political and religious intelligence units in state institutions and appointed its own trained officers, bureaucrats, and political elements to collect money from every corner of the country to facilitate its worldwide extremist and intelligence mission. Bureaucracy and leadership of the groups is composed of retired military generals and intelligence experts who have established worldwide contacts with governments, intelligence agencies and extremist organisations. Every Pakistani government and army chief is bound to facilitate this group, while civilian and military intelligence agencies have been sending their spy agents with its groups to every town, city, and province to collect intelligence information. Government of former Prime Minister Imran Khan and the Military establishment have been financially supporting Tablighi Jamaat since 2019, while the Punjab Assembly once passed a resolution in support of the group. In Britain, France, and the United States, the Tablighi Jamaat has appeared on the fringes of several terrorism investigations, leading some to speculate that its political stance simply masked fertile ground for breeding terrorism.

The group is the best source of intelligence collection for Pakistan and some Western intelligence agencies. Hindustan Times (Pakistan stood in support of Tablighi Jamaat, is Imran Khan going against Saudi Arabia? 24 December 2021) reported Pakistan's resolution in support of Tablighi Jamaat. The government of Saudi has already banned Tablighi Jamaat. In the assembly of Punjab province, the most influential province of Pakistan, the legislators have even passed a resolution in support of the Tablighi Jamaat. "During this, MLA Khadija Umar presented a proposal in support of Tablighi Jamaat. The Speaker read out the motion and said that the House agrees with the people promoting trust. He claimed that Tablighi Jamaat has nothing to do with terrorism and their history proves that they have never been involved in such work. Later, the motion was passed unanimously by the House. The newspaper reported. Hindustan Times reported the Saudi Arabia decision that the group was the entry point of terrorism and threatens society. The Saudi Ministry of Islamic Affairs instructed mosques to warn people not to join them in Friday prayers. In a series of tweets, the ministry said that His Excellency the Minister of Islamic Affairs, Dr. Abdullatif Al-Alsheikh, urged all mosques to include it in their rituals and to make people aware of the dangers associated with it".[28]

The presence of Tablighi Jamaat in the EU needs to be strictly monitored to avoid the possibility of a bigger bang. Networks of terrorist and extremist organizations in Europe are expanding with the arrival of new extremist elements and those who fought in Afghanistan, Iraq and Syria. The group represents military establishments of some states and their intelligence infrastructure, and works for the interests of some international intelligence agencies. Fear and terror marketing systems are updated every year and new techniques of destruction are being introduced. The way the Afghan Taliban design their strategies for training and brainwashing suicide bombers is not quite different from the suicide techniques of the ISIS-K.

# Chapter 3

# Intelligence Reform, Oversight Mechanism and the Role of CNCTR - National Commission and Democratic Accountability

The greatest threat to the national security of France stems from the business of nuclear smuggling and state sponsored terror groups operating in South Asia and Europe. The prospect of nuclear terrorism in Europe and possibly in France, is crystal clear as members of the Islamic State (ISIS) in Brussels tried to retrieve material for a dirty bomb. The risk of a complete nuclear device falling into the hands of terrorists will cause consternation in the country. Nuclear terrorism also remains a constant threat to global peace. Access of terrorist organizations to nuclear material is a bigger threat to the civilian population. The Edward Snowden leaks challenged policy makers and the public understanding and perspectives on the role of security intelligence in liberal democratic states. The persisting imbalance of power in the European Union states, intelligence war of foreign agencies on their soils, and the noticeably tilting power have made the continent feel vulnerable. National Security threat perception and countering foreign espionage strategies in every EU member state were diversified while their response to international terrorism flattered underwhelming. Over the past 20 years, growing national security controversies mostly revolved around the failure of intelligence cooperation among the EU member states, which resulted in mistrust and the emergence of major extremist organizations that threatened national security of the region. The introduction of Mass Surveillance programs of European intelligence services prompted anxiety and fear of warrantless information collection.

We live in an era of fear market where only ignorance drives our thoughts and responses every day. We observe many incidents of auctions in terror markets across the globe, in which innocent children are being sold for suicide terrorism. These are spreading successfully because we do not do our homework and we have no specific counterterrorism strategy. In India,

Europe, Pakistan and Afghanistan, the terror market is viewed in different perspectives. If we deeply study the news stories of suicide terror-related incidents, we will find that terrorists use different techniques in their attacks. The method of destruction and killing is the same but techniques and strategies are different. Terrorist organisations such as ISIS, and the Taliban through Facebook, YouTube and twitter invite young people to join their networks by using various marketing techniques. These terror groups are marketers as well as consumers to a degree; their recruiters 'market' boys and use them as human bombs against civil society and military infrastructure. They supply suicide bombers across Asia and the Middle East very cheap. Religious and political vendettas are being settled by using suicide bombers against rival groups or families. This generation of fear and panic is controlled by extremist elements and non-state actors. Fear and terror marketing systems are updated every year and new techniques of destruction are being introduced. European intelligence cooperation is in crisis as the majority of member states do not share their national secrets.

The EU maintains numerous institutions, networks, and databases for collaboration and intelligence sharing with partner services. In a rapidly changing environment, Intelligence Surveillance developed through different types of technologies, software, strategies and drones operations in Europe and the United Kingdom. There are various forms of surveillance mechanisms, including Human Agents, Computer Programs, and Global Positioning Satellite Devices. These surveillance devices are now even encroaching into the personal domain of the individuals without the knowledge of the individual being watched. In a surveillance state, people live in consternation, fear, and struggling to protect their privacy, family life, business secrets, and data. In a short period of time, it has amassed a rather sordid history of citizen surveillance–and it continues to be unlawful. Technological evolution and aggrandized interlinkage of our world in general, and specifically information technology, has affected people and society in different ways. Daily life of every man and woman has become influenced by these challenges. The twenty-first century appeared with different classes of National Security threats.

After the first decade, world leaders, research scholars, journalists, politicians, and security experts grasped that the world has become the most dangerous place. The avoidance of war was the primary objective of superpowers, but with the end of the Cold War, emergence of Takfiri Jihadism, extremism, and terrorism prompted many unmatched challenges. Home-grown extremism and radicalization continues to expose a significant threat to the National Security of the EU member states. The risks from state-based threats have both grown and diversified. The unmethodical and impulsive use of a military-grade nerve agent on British soil is the worst unlawful act of bioterrorists. The dynamics of Taliban legitimacy, and their disputed leadership, however, is not out of the way from other powerful terrorist groups, such as ISIS, Lashkar-e-Taiba and Central Asian groups. These external actors may also influence the relationship between Taliban and Afghan civilians. Taliban's way of governance has taken place under the conditions of civil war. They have adopted a culture of violence and jihad against the education of Afghan girls.[1]

There are debates in some intellectual circles in London that foreign intelligence interference in France has established secret units in remote areas clean of CCTV and police visibility. The reason for this is that these agencies operate in cities with impunity. French intelligence agencies and parliamentarians have already warned that Chinese intelligence agencies were making things worse. French counter espionage Director, Mr. Nicolas Lerner, provided an overview of the current situation in front of a parliamentary committee of inquiry on foreign interference. Expert and writer, Jacques Follorou in his Le Monde newspaper analysis (Le Monde April 27, 2023) noted statement of the head of French Counter-Intelligence, Mr. Nicolas Lerner, in front of the parliamentary committee of inquiry into political, economic and financial interference by foreign powers: "This committee was established on 06 December 2022, chaired by MP Jean-Philippe Tanguy The head of the General Directorate for Internal Security (DGIS) was questioned behind closed doors. "Since I have been in charge of this service since 2018, we've detected efforts by certain intelligence officers to make approaches targeting the entire political spectrum," Mr. Lerner noted.[2] He also stated that individual approaches are happening and some people have been able to enter into relationships not allowed under French law. He stated; "I do have some examples in mind." The head of the DGSI warned that once he had detected contacts with Russian intelligence officers under diplomatic cover."[3]

Writers, Gérard Davet and Fabrice Lhomme (The French secret service and its 'war chest' caught in the nets of the justice system, Le Monde, January 11, 2023) have raised the question of the hidden face of the French foreign intelligence agency.[4] If an intelligence agency lives in shadow, its social and professional influence in society is shrunken.[5] After the Paris terrorist attacks, the French Parliament designed legal strategies by overhauling the legal framework for intelligence surveillance mechanism. France maintains a strong and professional intelligence infrastructure that experienced and lived through different phases of World War I and II, and the extensive Cold War period. Its share with different EU intelligence agencies on law enforcement level is considered indispensable and critical. The establishment of the National Commission (CNCTR) for the control of intelligence techniques in 2015 was the doorstep to the introduction of all around and wide-ranging security sector reform in France. States in Europe were forced to react quickly amidst rapidly changing geopolitical circumstances. Experts Davide Basso and Pekka Vanttinen in their analysis (France threatened by Russian spies 'under diplomatic cover'-EURACTIV, 28 April 2023), have raised the question of Russian interference in the internal affairs of France. France was particularly exposed to the interference of Russian agencies as Nicolas Lerner, the head of the General Directorate for Internal Security (DGSI) has noted in his report. Head of the DGSI, Mr. Lerner, warned about political interference and the importance of disinformation in undermining France's voice.[6]

French politics is complex and indiscernible. In my book (The UK Big-3), I documented foreign intelligence interference in Denmark, Sweden, Norway and Northern European states. The present riots in France abruptly became violent and the way they countered the police and law enforcement agencies, the way rioters demonstrated in a mysterious way of destruction, show that it was not a protest only but the country was so badly punished by foreign intelligence agencies and radicalized groups. We know French intelligence infrastructure is a professional and competent one, but representations of different cultures and political stakeholders within the law enforcement agencies make things worse. There are many holes that facilitate foreign spy networks infiltration into French society. France needs one more competent and Professional Counterintelligence Agency to check the operational mechanism of existing agencies. Ten days of rioting across France have once again exposed the country's acute social tensions at a time of growing political polarization. The latest protests demonstrate that France's impoverished, ethnically-mixed neighbourhoods remain a powder keg, riven with a feeling of injustice, racial discrimination and abandonment by the state. The rioting is a reminder of the deep-seated social and economic problems in France's poorer districts and the long legacy of government neglect.[7]

Open Democracy in its report (France's surveillance: justice, freedom and security in the EU. Nicholas Hernanz, Julien Jeandesboz, Joanna Parkin, Francesco Ragazzi, Amandine Scherrer, Didier Bigo and Sergio Carrera- 14 May 2014) has noted some aspects of reforms and surveillance mechanism in France. The Magazine article noted that France has been constantly improving its intelligence infrastructure since 2008. The DGSE has further developed its intelligence expertise to fight sarcastic elements effectively. Reportedly, France's communications surveillance and collection architecture rest primarily on a supercomputer operated by the DGSE in Paris".[8]In July 2023, the French government authorized the police and law enforcement agencies to surreptitiously use mobile phones and other devices as their own surveillance tools. The provision, sanctioned on 05 July 2023, permitted police to remotely activate the cameras, microphones, and GPS of suspects' phones, laptops, cars, and other connected devices.[9]

On 01 June 2023, the European Parliament endorsed a report on countering foreign interference and information manipulation, calling for a whole-of-society approach to tackling the issue. The report advocated, in particular, for a move away from what it said was the "country-agnostic" approach to tackling foreign interference and information manipulation (FIMI) currently practiced by the Commission and the European External Action Service. For weeks, terrorists and extremists were burning Police stations, libraries, schools, buildings and even targeted national critical infrastructure. A parliamentary report on foreign interference in France, highlighted China's growing interference. Expert and journalist John Keiger (The French riots threaten the state's very existence, Spectator Magazine, 02 July 2023) highlighted the present civil war in the mirror of 2021 Islamic terrorism:

"Go back two years to April 2021 and the wake of Islamic terrorism and 'gilets jaunes' riots. Twenty generals, a hundred mostly retired senior officers and a thousand military personnel signed a strident letter in the right-wing French weekly Valeurs actuelles addressed to the president, the government and parliamentarians. 'The hour is grave, France is in peril, and several mortal dangers threaten it.' It stated that members of the army would not stand idly by while French values were trampled by anti-racist doctrines, no-go areas and mob-rule. It appealed for 'honor to be restored to our rulers' and warned of 'disintegration' of French society as a result of government policy: 'there is no time for prevarication, if not, tomorrow civil war will put an end to the mounting chaos, and the deaths, whose responsibility will be yours, will be counted in their thousands'. (John Keiger,

The French riots threaten the state's very existence, The Spectator-02 July 2023).[10] The Yellow Vests Protests were also a series of extremists dance in France that began on 17 November 2018. At first the protestors advocated economic justice, later they called for institutional political reforms. On 29 November 2018, a list of 42 demands was made public and went viral on social media, becoming a de facto structuring basis for the movement. The demands covered a wide range of eclectic topics, mostly related to democracy, and social and fiscal justice."[11]

The real issue of foreign espionage needed to be addressed through security sector reform within the European Union and France, because without SSR, countering foreign espionage is impossible. The Danish intelligence, Sweden, Norway and Finland intelligence infrastructures suffered huge failure when reports of Iranian and Chinese intelligence interference appeared in newspapers and social media. Iranian and Chinese intelligence agencies had established recruitment centres in these states where educated people were being recruited to collect information of Iranian interests. China also spread its blanket to teach some lessons to its cronies. China and Iran were spying on EU embassies, the Defence Department and the intelligence infrastructure of Denmark, according to the Danish intelligence report (PET Report) that uncovered espionage networks of Iran, China, and Russia in Denmark to recruit people from different segments of society.

As mentioned earlier, the European Union has been facing the threat of foreign espionage networks since 2001. Immediately after the US attacks. But policy makers and intelligence stakeholders have raised questions about the weak and contradictory approach of member states towards countering these networks. Some have remarked that an intelligence without reform cannot counter and cannot contain any suspicious activity of foreign sponsored spy agencies, and some understand that man power and modern espionage technology can play a crucial role against these sarcastic elements. The French secret services have the capacity to counter terrorism and extremism with its modern intelligence technology. Intelligence failed on many occasions, but we can judge the recent riots and violent protests of extremist and radicalized forces that intelligence wasn't failed, the policing forces failed due to their lack of coordination with other agencies. The Ukraine war has been a good opportunity for the EU, particularly French secret agencies to review its security approach, operational capabilities and counterterrorism strategies, in order to make its infrastructure competent and professional. Expert Michael Jonsson (Expert Michael Jonsson-11

September 2023) has reviewed counterintelligence in post-cold war Europe:

"To date there is no comparable study of espionage in contemporary Europe. Instead, there are a handful of comparative articles analysing large-N samples of espionage within individual jurisdictions, at different periods in time. For instance, Jurvee and Perling published a survey of Russian espionage cases in Estonia. The sample includes 20 individuals convicted during 2009–2019, of which all but one were male. Three convicts had a background from the Estonian Internal Security Service (ISS) and one was an army officer, and these four individuals received notably harsher sentencing than the rest of the sample, presumably reflecting the gravity of their betrayal. Lillbacka studied 285 cases compiled from Finland (1945–1977), Sweden (1939–1942) and the U.S. (1975–2008), to test statistically the proposition that ideologically motivated spies 'originate primarily from socio-culturally coherent groups where beliefs that are directly or indirectly favourable to a foreign power are prevalent'.... Most notably, in the 1990–2015 period, China overtook Russia as the main instigator of espionage against the US. In Europe, Russia instead remained the by far greatest instigator, responsible for 37 out of 42 cases. In the 32 Russian cases where it was possible to pinpoint a specific security service, the GRU (14 individuals) and the FSB (15) were the most prolific, whereas SVR was responsible for only three recruitments....Hence, while Chinese espionage against Europe is ascendant–and receives increasing counterintelligence attention – Russia to date remains the main instigator behind cases that have led to court convictions in Europe."[12]

Some observers and experts in Europe view the decrease in Russian intelligence interference may be due to the country's engagement in the war with Ukraine, but it doesn't mean Russian is not closely watching Europe. Normally, every state has a moral obligation to protect its interests abroad. The same Russia is doing in Europe. After the war in Ukraine started in 2022, the issue of EU sanctions against Russia became an important topic of intellectual forums in Europe. The EU, US, UK, and other states imposed sweeping sanctions to support peace and the territorial integrity of Ukraine, but things got worse. In the European Council in June 2023, the project categorically said that it condemned Russian aggression against Ukraine that constitutes a manifest violation of the UN Charter. Expert and analyst John Psaropoulos in his Al Jazeera news analysis (Europe awakens to the threat of sabotage by Russian agents, Al Jazeera 17 Jan 2023) noted that member states of European Union have now awakened to the threat of Russian intelligence threat:

"Suspicion has fallen on Russia over a series of confirmed or apparent acts of sabotage and espionage that took place late last year in Western Europe, experts say, with European countries increasingly taking measures in response. On October 19, internet cables were severed in the south of France at three locations simultaneously. Cloud Security Company Zscaler said the cable cuts, which severed digital highways linking Marseille with Lyon, Barcelona and Milan, had "impacted major cables with connectivity to Asia, Europe, US and potentially other parts of the world".... "By all available accounts, Russian espionage Unit 29155 has been in existence since at least 2009. It consists of a small number of personnel, possibly around 200, with an additional 20-40 operations officers," said Joseph Fitsanakis, professor of intelligence and security studies at Coastal Carolina University. Fitsanakis told Al Jazeera that the unit has its origins in networks of Soviet agents who "were at times tasked with developing and maintaining plans for large-scale sabotage, behind enemy lines, which would become operational during a conventional war between the USSR and the West. They included acts of sabotage against energy networks, public utilities, civilian or military harbours, telecommunications systems."[13]

These are the west and Europe perceptions about Russian intelligence, while Russian has repudiated these allegations and said the US and Europe has destroyed Nord Stream-2 Pipeline. Traditionally, intelligence was not conceived in France as a functional tool in the hands of the decision-maker but was rather defined as an array. Secret spying activities were driven from its concept of state security. The present intelligence reform generated debate in intellectual circles that it is an effort to reorganize the French intelligence infrastructure, create a strong coordination between law enforcement agencies. 'The idea of a French 'exceptionalism' is addressed through a theoretical approach of the way France redefines intelligence and surveillance in relation with a major evolution of the notion of 'reason of State' itself…This reform is based on processes of rationalisation, centralization, modernisation and normalisation of both intelligence activities and intelligence services in France'. (Intelligence reform and the transformation of the state: the end of a French exception. Olivier Chopin-22 May 2017).[14]

In France, politicians have long been advocating a strong accountability and oversight system, and publishing their statements in newspapers. Expert Damien Van Puyvelde (Intelligence, Democratic Accountability, and the Media in France-21 Aug 2014) noted relationship of intelligence and media in France: "The recent affaire des fadettes—in which the Central Directorate for Domestic Intelligence tapped a journalist's phone to trace the source of an unauthorized disclosure of government information— epitomizes the precarious position of the press in France. Following recent reforms, the French system of intelligence accountability would benefit from a more collaborative relationship between the institutions of government and the media. The lack of academic interest in intelligence in France partly explains the prevalence of many preconceived ideas about French Intelligence."[15]Now, the question is how to counter hybrid threat within the European Union member states and how to professionalize their intelligence infrastructures to effectively counter extremism, radicalization and foreign espionage networks. Expert Susana Sanz-Caballero (The concepts and laws applicable to hybrid threats, with a special focus on Europe. Humanities & Social Sciences Communications journal-29 June 2023) has defined the concept of hybrid threat that pose risk to states:

"Hybrid threats pose a real risk to states because their objective is to destabilise the adversary through ever increasing means and tactics, which are not easy to detect ... .Nevertheless, it is difficult to confront threats if we do not know what these phenomena are or anything about their configurations. Even so, malign asymmetric threats are on the rise and so states and international organisations are being forced to start considering what actions they might use to counter them. It is therefore important to agree upon a definition of hybrid threats that is broad enough to include as wide a range of means of state destabilisation as possible..... Thus, hybrid threats consist of political activities, (dis)informational campaigns, and cyber, military, economic, and societal interventions. Moreover, although cyber-based threats are polemic, they represent only one of the domains in which hybrid threats may occur. Indeed, the 'weapons' used in the grey zone could include computers, border gates, fake news, drones, cyber-troll farms, radio stations, hijacked aircraft or ships, and spy balloons crossing into airspace not belonging to its jurisdiction of origin".1 Political demonstrations, disinformation demonstration and cyber activities are included in hybrid threat to states those are weak and in turmoil.[16]

French intelligence was implicated in a multifaceted crisis, while if we look at its past historical status, it has been a competent agency during the First and Second World Wars, and extensive Cold War. In his Aljazeera analysis, Bruce Crumley (Were the Paris attacks a French intelligence failure? Al Jazeera November 17, 2015) has argued that the Paris attacks occurred due to the intelligence failure but some experts say that was due to the police failure. The Paris attacks generated different stories of police failure to intercept terrorists entering Paris. "An investigative committee of France's Parliament announced that it had found intelligence lapses leading up to the November terror attacks in Paris. Georges Fenech, head of the Special Parliamentary Commission noted the Paris 2015 attacks: "Our intelligence services have failed. Research Scholar and expert, Shashank Joshi (Charlie Hebdo attack: A French intelligence failure? BBC 10 January 2015) in his analysis of the attacks of Paris and mismanagement of security system in France has noted that France had unusually powerful intelligence agencies."[17]

The French surveillance faced several challenges. Privacy concerns began to collide with national security interests, and policy makers needed to prepare for a new intelligence war. Edward Snowden exposed communication surveillance that triggered political debate. In addition to the government surveillance, private companies are also doing the same job in Paris, but their work and data are mostly contradictory and misleading. Cross border mobility of people, interoperability, interactivity and interface of different policing and intelligence agencies couldn't restore confidence of military establishments, intelligence leaders and law enforcement stakeholders. That clefts and misconstruction still exist. Scientific collaboration, joint ventures and interoperability of police and intelligence infrastructures, and mismanagement of border altercations, further caused miscalculation and mistrust. The process of intelligence sharing among the EU member states has been extremely underwhelming after Brexit. The UK security became vulnerable after its political and judicial separation from the EU project. Thus, Sweden, Finland, Estonia, Lithuania and Latvia jointly managed the flow of strategic and technical intelligence information and helped each other in fighting radicalization and extremism.

Privacy International (December, 2021) in its report noted strict surveillance measures of the EU to control population and maintain law and order, but this is not a rational panacea. Surveillance and secretly watching the civilian population and violating privacy cannot help maintain security.[18] 'Democratic states use surveillance technologies to facilitate governance through social control. (Surveillance Technology Challenges Political Culture of Democratic States. Inez Miyamoto)'.[19] The 2022 Strategic Compass sets out the EU's ambition to become a global leader in AI by reducing the dependency on external actors for emerging technologies, increasing the production of high-performance computer processors and the establishment of an independent data space'. (Artificial intelligence and EU security: the false promise of digital sovereignty. Andrea Calderaro & Stella Blumfelde).[20]

With the presence of Jihadist Groups and the ISIS members in France, the use of chemical, biological and nuclear weapons cannot be ruled out, the fact is, that the ISIS found these weapons in Iraq. Material of Dirty Bomb, biological and nuclear weapons material can be purchased from black market of India and Pakistan. There are possibilities that terrorists can acquire nuclear material or a complete warhead to use it against their targets. The risk of a complete nuclear device falling into the hands of terrorists will cause consternation in the EU. Over the past several years, the prospect of a terrorist group armed with nuclear and biological weapons has frequently been cited as a genuine and overriding threat to the security of Europe. Moreover, there are possibilities that Pakistan, Afghanistan and Africa based extremist and jihadist groups can purchase fissile material in black market or steal it from a military or civilian facility and then use that material to construct an improvised nuclear device.

ISIS found these kinds of dangerous weapons in Iraq and killed thousands of innocent women and children there. In France, there are several networks of extremist and terrorist groups that may possibly seek biological weapons to use against local security forces. Chechen extremist groups have also consistently expressed their desire to obtain, build, and utilize unconventional devices against selected targets, and have innovated by incorporating hazardous materials into their ordnance. The war in Ukraine, Syria, Afghanistan and Iraq has significantly altered modern terrorism, with radical Islamic militants from Africa being no exception. The terrorists' method for recruiting forces is almost the same in most of the countries in Africa and South Asia. While the majority of ISIS recruits originate in the Middle East, the Maghreb, and Western Europe. Central Asia is the third-largest source of foreign fighters in Syria.

Nuclear terrorism remains a constant threat to global peace. Access of terrorist organizations to nuclear material is a bigger threat to the civilian population in France. Terrorist groups can gain access to highly enriched uranium or plutonium, because they have the potential to create and detonate an improvised nuclear device. Since ISIS has already retrieved nuclear materials from Mosul city of Iraq, we can assert that terrorist groups like ISIS and Katibat Imam Bukhari, and Chechen extremist groups, AL Shabab and Boko Haram, can make access to biological and nuclear weapons with the help of local experts. Nuclear facilities also often store large amounts of radioactive material, spent fuel, and other nuclear waste products that terrorists could use in a dirty bomb. Without access to such fissile materials, extremist and radicalised groups can turn their attention toward building a simple radiological device. The most difficult part of making a nuclear bomb is acquiring the nuclear material, but some Muslim and non-Muslim states might facilitate ISIS, Lashkar-e-Taiba, Chechen extremist groups and Afghanistan and Pakistan based groups to attack nuclear installations in Europe.

For more than two decades, the threat of nuclear and biological terrorism has been at the forefront of the international security agenda. Nuclear experts have often warned that terrorists and extremist organisations operating in Europe must be prevented from gaining access to weapons of mass destruction and from perpetrating atrocious acts of nuclear terrorism. The greatest threat to the national security of Europe stems from nuclear smuggling and terror groups operating in different states. Terrorist groups will prefer to use biological weapons against their targets with low visibility, and this type of attack can be accomplished from a remote area. They could have up to two weeks of undetected operational lead time before local governments caught up with them. Analyst Charles D. Ferguson in his paper (Assessing Radiological Weapons: Attack Methods and Estimated Effects. Defence against Terrorism Review Vol. 2, No. 2, fall 2009) spotlighted clandestine relationship of terrorist groups with insiders within the government departments. He understands that radioactive material in a radiological weapon can come from many sources.

He also documented the storage of radioactive material in nuclear power plants, research reactor facilities, hospitals, blood banks, universities, food irradiation centres, oil well sites, and shipbuilding and construction sites are many of the major places where radioactive materials are used and stored. Some of these places are more vulnerable than others to terrorists obtaining radioactive material'. Governance and administratively protection of radioactive materials in the war zone of Ukraine is a highly challenging assignment for the contested governments and international community. This is particularly true for States suchlike Ukraine and Pakistan that have experienced conflict, including ethnic and armed civil war but still in control of large stockpiles of these weapons.[21] The problem of nuclear and biological terrorism deserves special attention from Russia and China as the IS-K and Central Asian groups want to develop capability of dirty bombs and use of biological weapons. The use of these weapons might have severe health effects, causing more disruption than destruction.

Political and military circles in Russia and China Pakistan fear that, as IS-K has already tested its power of seizing chemical weapons in Al Muthanna, in Northern Iraq, some disgruntled retired military officers or experts in nuclear explosive devices of some Muslim states might help the IS-K to deploy biological and chemical weapons.

The current instability in Ukraine, and Pakistan, presence of 31 terrorist groups in Taliban controlled Afghanistan and the ongoing Sunni insurgency in Iraq, has energized the African Salafi-jihadi groups based in Paris, and has emboldened their supporters to orchestrate large-scale casualty attacks in France. Recent media reports identified Moldovan criminal groups that attempted to smuggle radioactive materials to Daesh (also known as the Islamic State of Iraq and Syria, or ISIS) in 2015. In 2022, the new Taliban government brought together families of Afghan and Pakistani suicide bombers in a hotel and praised their suicide mission. Their sacrifices are for religion, for the country and for Islam, Mr. Haqqani told the crowd. Deputy Minister of information and culture and spokesperson of the Taliban Zabiullah Mujahid said that the battalion will be part of their special forces and will be active under the Defense Ministry. About women and former officers in the Taliban's army, Mujahid acknowledged that women will be recruited based on need, and specialists of the previous Afghan army will also be given a part in the future army. In view of the above painted pictures of fear, terrorism, suicide attacks and nuclear black marketing, the French government passed several professional security measures and strategies to make the security of the country and tackle all terrorist and extremist elements professionally. On 24 July 2015, the French Parliament passed a surveillance law to effectively monitor movement of anti-state elements. Terror attacks of Charlie Hebdo forces the government to adopt such a law. The law gave legal status to intelligence techniques that operated in the past without a legal framework.

# Chapter 4

# The French Major Intelligence and Law Enforcement Reforms: Legal Limitations and Surveillance

The abrupt outburst in towns and cities of France was a great lesson for all European states that managing a better law and order can be laborious without introducing security sector reforms. As we have seen in yesteryears, terrorist and extremist groups made access to nuclear sites and recruited a good number of European citizens in order to use them for jihad in Europe. From the Yellow Vest movement to the recent terrorism (riots) incidents, extremist forces had designed to take control of government installations, cities and towns in order to further strengthen their networks. Al Jazeera (02 Jul 2023) also reported the 2023 riots in which young rioters clashed with police overnight and targeted a mayor's home with a burning car. 'Police made arrests nationwide in an attempt to quell France's worst social upheaval in years. 'French Prime Minister Elisabeth Borne condemned the attack. "We will let no violence get by" unpunished, she said, urging that the perpetrators be sanctioned with the "utmost severity". Al Jazeera noted.[1] A Police officer fatally killed an African French national in June 2023 during the traffic stop. This incident caused unrest and demonstration of extremist elements who set fire to thousands of businesses across France. Violent demonstrations were reported in nearly 300 cities and towns around the country during this period.

Terrorist groups used modern technology and military-grade weapons to attack governments and private properties. Some extremist and terrorist elements have crossed borders from neighbouring states to help their groups members in looting, vandalism and fear marketing. In France more that 70 percent asylum seekers have submitted fake documents to the immigration departments-with their fake names and tribal affiliation. Terrorists and extremists are claiming asylum on fake documents from across the globe.

Intelligence challenges in Europe need a professional assessment to address issues of sharing, analysis, and process and information dissemination. By taking this step, policy makers must be purveyed processed intelligence information and they must be led in the right direction. "There is also some work on the typology of the intelligence problem as a whole, (Christiaan Menkveld. Understanding the complexity of intelligence problems-08 Feb 2021).[2] There is also quite some work on the application of complex adaptive systems on the field of international relations. Associate researcher at CNRS and post-doctoral researcher at CERI Sciences in Paris, Felix Treguer in his paper (Major oversight gaps in the French intelligence legal framework. 25 March 2022) has noted surveillance techniques of French intelligence, and also highlighted parliamentary and legal oversight of agencies:

"In 2021, French Government introduced major intelligence and law enforcement reforms to make its intelligence infrastructure, but some issues have not been highlighted in detail, suchlike intelligence dissemination, sharing, open source surveillance and international standard of intelligence oversight. Experts stressed the need for legal and parliamentary oversight and coordination of intelligence agencies with law enforcement agencies. Revelations of Edward Snowden forced the French parliament to pass an intelligence revision act after the 2015 terrorist attacks in Paris. The reform passed in 2016 is certainly much less ambitious than its 2015 predecessor. Yet, strengthening oversight should be a priority, given the role of intelligence in government. Since 2015, French intelligence agencies have seen their workforce increase by 30 percent, in particular to develop their technological capabilities. In this context, the use of various surveillance techniques have increased significantly, in particular in areas that are especially sensitive for civil rights. For instance, following criticisms by civil society organisations during the parliamentary debate in 2015, the CNCTR has warned in several annual reports about an important oversight gap regarding the sharing of data between French intelligence services and foreign agencies"[3]

Legal system of France on intelligence surveillance is also silent. The French law also views open surveillance differently, especially twitter and Facebook. In France, transparency is difficult to be judged notwithstanding the CNCTR in its report claimed accuracy of information. Associate researcher at CNRS and post-doctoral researcher at CERI Sciences in Paris, Felix Treguer in his paper (Major oversight gaps in the French intelligence legal framework. 25. March 2022) has noted weaknesses of transparency and accuracy of intelligence information: "In France, such a degree of transparency seems unimaginable for the moment. Even if the CNCTR has made some progress in the accuracy of the information it provides in its reports, it often sticks to mere descriptions of the state of the law and its evolution, or issues general statistics on the types of measures authorised and their purposes. This is still a far cry from the level of detail feeding the public debate and the work of parliamentarians, journalists or NGOs in countries such as the United Kingdom or Germany. French law also makes no mention of so-called open source surveillance, especially on social networks such as Facebook or Twitter – an activity about which little has been leaked to the press but known to have grown in importance over the last ten years."[4]

The secret intelligence watchdog in its annual report noted that parliamentarians were pointing to the fact that the oversight system was weak. Journalist Jacques Follorou in his recent report (Intelligence-gathering: French oversight board alarmed by the rise in requests concerning political activism. Le Monde 16 June, 2023), critically discussed the surveillance system in France and the CNCTR monitoring of the French intelligence agencies. He also noted that this body was now seriously concerned about its professional approach to intelligence technology operations. "The CNCTR describes itself as an organization employing 20th-century surveillance techniques while endeavouring to keep an eye on 21st-century technology. It also highlighted the doctrinal void left by the French authorities on key issues such as political activism. Jacques Follorou noted.[5] Associate researcher at CNRS and post-doctoral researcher at CERI Sciences in Paris, expert Félix Tréguer in his analysis (Major oversight gaps in the French intelligence legal framework-25. March 2022) noted that in 2021, the French government passed a security sector and intelligence surveillance reform bill which was criticised by politicians. He also noted that after the Edward Snowden revelations, the French government passed a revised intelligence act:

"Eight years after the revelations of whistle-blower Edward Snowden, the French Parliament passed the first major revision of the Intelligence Act. Initially adopted right after the Paris attacks of January 2015, this piece of legislation was at the time presented by the rapporteur of the bill at the National Assembly, Jean-Jacques Urvoas, as a "progress in the rule of law." But such framing obscured an important fact: the reform legalised surveillance measures that had been used for years in complete illegality, which should have led to criminal prosecutions against the political and administrative leaders who had authorised these programs. The reform passed last year is certainly much less ambitious than its 2015 predecessor. However, it follows the same logic, well analysed by sociologists Laurent Bonelli, Hervé Rayner and Bernard Voutat, which consists in using the law to legitimise the action of the services and preserve their room for manoeuvre. Accordingly, the law provided legal backing for increasingly extensive surveillance capabilities–such as "black boxes" that scan Internet traffic to detect "suspicious" URLs (Article 13), data sharing between French agencies (Article 7), or the obligation for private tech companies to collaborate with the authorities to hack encrypted messaging (Article 10), while at the same time sheltering the services from strong oversight".[6]

Terrorist attacks in Germany, France and Brussels forced several members of the European Union to introduce intelligence and security sector reforms. In 2002, the Joint Situation Centre started to be a forum for exchanging of intelligence information among France, Germany, Italy, the Netherlands, Spain, Sweden and the United Kingdom. Majority of European Union states introduced strict surveillance measures to collect data by legal means. There is voluminous and billowing material in case of books, journals, and newspaper and research papers on European intelligence surveillance, available in libraries and markets that highlight violation of privacy and private life of citizens of all EU member states. On the Internet, we can find important research papers on the decisions of the EU Court of Human Rights against the human right violations in blanket surveillance. The EU has been accused of contributing to the development of 'surveillance' capacities in third countries without considering fundamental rights.

Now, I want to lay down some sentences about the intelligence reform of Germany where the crisis of surveillance caused trust deficit and lack of public confidence about the approach of security stakeholders. In Europe, particularly in Germany, newspapers and journals published several articles and papers, while some newspapers published interviews of security experts to inculcate the stakeholders that this way of surveillance is causing alienation and torment among civil society. In some of my books, I have already highlighted criticism on German intelligence (BND) and the reform packages, recent analysis of experts of Digital rights, surveillance, and democracy in the Stiftung Neue Verantwortung, Kilian Vieth and intelligence expert Dr. Thorsten who heads Stiftung Neue Verantwortung's research on surveillance and democratic governance. (Five things you didn't know about Germany's foreign intelligence reform, 23. March 2022) has revealed some new things that forced me to add it to my analysis:

"The latest, but by no means last, episode in Germany's SIGINT policy-making process resulted in the Bundestag's adoption of a whole new set of complex provisions and exceptions. It is easy to get lost in the intricacies and cross-references of the amended Act of 2021. It is now (mostly) in force and includes an expanded mandate for strategic bulk interception, computer network exploitation and transnational data sharing of Germany's foreign intelligence agency, the BND (see our in-depth analysis here)....If the Bundesnachrichtendienst (BND) wants to collect foreign communications from a mobile network or internet service provider (ISP) based in Germany, it may legally compel the company to cooperate and facilitate access to the required data. But what about accessing data from communications providers that are not subject to German jurisdiction? Naturally, the data held by foreign providers is often of great interest to the BND, considering that its mission is to collect relevant information about foreign and security policy around the globe. As the German SIGINT agency cannot legally compel a foreign company that holds or routes the data to provide access, the new legal basis now explicitly allows the BND to secretly infiltrate foreign providers".[7]

This change in the BND Act cannot protect phone social media users from the agency reach. The BND surveillance in the presence of a clear government's guidance has reached beyond limitations. Both experts have documented several important legal limitations, some of which legally allow the agency to hack computer systems. The experts have raised a question of the overhaul of the legal framework for German intelligence that caused loopholes. Germany again changed its foreign intelligence framework in 2021. The new law has signal intelligence authorization of hacking foreign ISPs. In 2020, a German court made a decision about the country's foreign intelligence surveillance carried out by the Federal Intelligence Service. Federal commissioner for data protection and freedom of information analysis of the country viewed the draft of the Federal Intelligence Services Act (BNDG), while in 2020, the constitutional court decided the key provisions in the persisting legal framework about the BND were unconstitutional. Germany reformed its foreign intelligence four times: 2016 first post-Snowden BND reform, 2020 landmark constitutional court judgement, 2020 pre-legislative scrutiny proceedings and 2021 second BND reform. Expert of German intelligence, Ulrich Kelber, in his recent analysis of German legal framework (Aspects where Germany's draft Federal Intelligence Services Act misses the mark-16, February 2021), has critically highlighted the BND and its surveillance mechanism:

"The draft BNDG permits the transfer of intelligence obtained by strategic surveillance for the purpose of political information of the Federal Government to other domestic intelligence and law enforcement authorities. This contradicts the Court's findings, according to which such data is strictly restricted for the purpose of information of the highest level of the Federal Government in order to prepare government decisions. According to the Court, such data may be transferred to other authorities with operative competences only under very restricted circumstances, inter alia a threat to life. Even the Federal Government is not allowed to transfer this information to subordinate agencies for other, particularly operational, purposes. In addition, the draft BNDG neither meets the requirements by the Constitutional Court on transfers of data obtained through strategic surveillance of foreign telecommunications to national intelligence, police and law enforcement authorities for purposes of early threat detection (which is the second purpose besides political information justified by the Court to conduct strategic surveillance by the BND), nor does it meet the constitutional requirements for transfers of data obtained through CNE for this purpose. According to the Court's finding, the transfer of personal data from strategic surveillance of foreign telecommunications to "other bodies", which includes national intelligence services and law enforcement authorities, are justified only to protect highly important legal interests and require as a threshold for transfers the presence of a "concretised threat" or, in the case of transfers for law enforcement purposes, a "sufficiently concretised suspicion of crime".[6] Germany reformed its foreign intelligence four times. The 2016 first post-Snowden BND reform, 2020 landmark constitutional court judgement, 2020 pre-legislative scrutiny proceedings and 2021 second BND reform.[7]

The German Foreign Intelligence (BND) Act was amended in 2021, which caused anxiety among the Court of Justice of the European Union (CJEU) , the Independent Oversight Council (UKR) and several human rights organizations. The German Constitutional Court's landmark's judgment on the BND Act has been the sole reference point in public discussions. On 06 October 2020, the European Union Court of Justice passed on two judgements, in which stern limits on the power of BND to have an access to personal data. A Jean Monnet Professor ad personam in law at Queen Mary University of London and Emeritus Professor at Radboud University, Nijmegen, Netherlands, expert Elspeth Guild and head of Stiftung Neue Verantwortung's research on surveillance and democratic governance, Intelligence expert, Thorsten Wetzlingin their legal analysis (Germany's

BND Act & recent CJEU case law, 17. February 2021-About Intel) has noted different judgments on the power of BND:

"In the QdN judgment, the CJEU requires an effective review by a court or by an independent administrative body. This language is close to that of the European Court of Human Rights, the decisions of which must be taken into account by EU courts when determining the scope of rights which appear in both the EU Charter and the European Convention on Human Rights. The Human Rights Court has frequently been required to determine the characteristics necessary for an effective review. It has avoided accepting the title given by states to bodies charged with reviewing security services in favour of a functional definition based on the body's composition, powers, and scope of action. We now point readers to sections 23, 42, and 51 of the draft BND Act. These provisions, in particular, speak to the mandate, powers, and scope of action of the envisaged UKR. Notice that the UKR would consist of two separate branches, one for the judicial authorisation and related decisions (see sections 42-49) and another for the administrative review of data processing and other activities (see sections 50-52). Following the judgment of the German Constitutional Court, both entities of the UKR are designed to perform "legality control" (Rechtskontrolle), something Karlsruhe found significantly underwhelming and partly absent in the current legislation".[8]

In Germany, France and Eastern European states, intelligence oversight must work on internal level, executive and parliamentary level to make sure intelligence is transparently purveyed to policy makers and law enforcement agencies. Interoperability of law enforcement agencies, and intelligence operation has now become extremely important in epoch of intelligence war, and military conflicts in Ukraine. Development of military and artificial intelligence technologies, scientific collaboration and interoperability between European police and intelligence agencies, has brought the EU member states to a close. Collaboration among Sweden, Finland, Ukraine, Estonia, Lithuania, Poland and Latvia to manage flow of strategic and technological intelligence and information on law enforcement level to fight crimes and foreign intelligence infiltration. Writer Justine Victoria Valentin in her master thesis on Peace and Conflict Transformation (the Polarization of French society: a study of the Yellow Vests movement, SVF-3901. Faculty of Humanities, Social Science, and Education. Center for Peace Studies-May 2022).[9] On November 17th, 2018, French people, wearing a yellow security vest, came together in the streets of the big cities and on the roundabouts of the country towns. This movement stood out as particularly violent, on the part of the Yellow Vests, especially in Paris, and by severe repression on the part of the government. What was then called the Yellow Vests movement highlighted Social Polarization, as Structural Violence patterns.

In Eastern European states, the former Communist culture of intelligence is yet so strongly rooted in society and resists all new efforts of bringing intelligence under democratic control. In Greece, Lithuania, Estonia, Ukraine, Romania, and Poland, private, political, and bureaucratic stakeholders have generated numerous problems. By law, all EU member states need to regulate organizations of their country's intelligence services and establish different units to divide responsibilities between military and civilian agencies.[10] The DW New report (15 May 2020) noted a revised bill on reform of the German domestic intelligence agency to boost liaison with regional authorities.[11] Electronic Frontier Foundation (14 January 2020) in its comprehensive report noted legal developments on the evaluating of intelligence act that entrust BND wide-ranging surveillance authority: "In 2016, Germany's Bundestag passed intelligence reform that many argued did not go far enough. Under the post-2016 order, an independent panel oversees the BND and any foreign intelligence collected from international communications networks must be authorized by the chancellor. However, the new reform explicitly allowed surveillance to be conducted on EUstates and institutions for the purpose of "foreign policy and security," and permitted the BND to collaborate with the NSA—both of which allow for the privacy of foreign individuals to be invaded. It is worth noting that part of what allows a case like this to move forward is the ability of German citizens to know more about the surveillance programs their nation operates".[12]

European Union governance faces a fundamental implementation dilemma. On the one hand, calls for effective EU policies are manifold and have increased over time. As a result, the EU has developed a vast body of law, covering a wide span of established policy areas. The annual report 2021 of Danish Security and Intelligence Services, Published by the Danish Intelligence Oversight Board-May 2022, has noted responsibilities of the Denmark's intelligence: "the Danish Security and Intelligence Service (DSIS) is tasked with the main responsibility of acting as: National intelligence and security service, national security authority, and IT security authority under the Ministry of Justice. The Danish intelligence agencies have been tasked to 'prevent, investigate and counter operations and activities that pose or may pose a threat to freedom, democracy and safety in Danish society. Through its activities, DSIS must thus provide the basis for ensuring that threats of the said nature are identified and addressed as quickly and effectively as possible and, being part of the police, DSIS' essential objective is to work not only for overall safety, security, peace and order in society but also for the safety and security of each individual.[13]

Danish intelligence infrastructure suffered huge failure when reports of Iranian and Chinese intelligence appeared in newspapers and social media. Iranian and Chinese intelligence agencies had established recruitment centres where educated people were being recruited to collect information of Iranian interests. China also spread its blanket to teach some lessons to its caderads. China and Iran were spying on EU embassies, the defence department and intelligence infrastructure of Denmark. The Danish intelligence report (PET Report) uncovered espionage networks of Iran, China, and Russia in Denmark to recruit people from different segments of society. The PET report warned: "threat from foreign state intelligence activities targeting Denmark and Danish interests abroad presents our society with a number of significant political, security-related and economic challenges. In recent years, PET has uncovered several cases that illustrated how a number of foreign states were actively carrying out intelligence activities against Denmark. The authorities in other western countries had also uncovered cases of foreign espionage indicating the presence of a threat to their societies. PET assessed the threat from foreign state intelligence activities in Denmark was specific and persistent. The activities include espionage, influence operations, harassment, attempts to illegally procure products, technology and knowledge and, in exceptional cases, outright assassination attempts.[14]

The Denmark military intelligence Chief was jailed for sharing sensitive intelligence information with foreign intelligence agencies. On 12 January 2022, analyst Charles Szumski noted (Danish military intelligence chief jailed for espionage-EURACTIV.com) that Lars Findsen was jailed for a month for leaking classified documents to Danish media. "I plead not guilty," the head of Danish military intelligence admitted before the judge rendered his verdict.[15] On 9 December, the Danish authorities announced, without revealing their identity, the arrest of four former or current members of the kingdom's two intelligence services. Among other things, they were accused of disclosing "highly confidential information from the intelligence services without authorisation". Expert Nikita Belukhin (The Scandal in Denmark's Military Intelligence: Too Much Transparency? Modern Diplomacy, 25 March 2022) highlighted issue of espionage in

Denmark: "The delay in the key five military projects under the 2018-2023 Defence Agreement, including full meaning of the heavy mechanized 1st brigade in the amount of 4000 people, known as the 'fist of the army' and especially, the scandal permeating the Military Intelligence Services of Denmark, which allegedly carried out espionage against German, Dutch, France, Swedish and Norwegian colleagues in favour of the US National Security Agency, have not improved Denmark's standing in alliance either".[16]

The Danish Intelligence Oversight Board in its annual report, has explained the legal framework of the Danish Security and Intelligence Service (DSIS) Act and orders that were amended on different occasions: "The Danish Security and Intelligence Service (DSIS) Act (Consolidated Act No. 231 of 7 March 2017, as amended (most recently by Act No. 1706 of 27 December 2018)) (the DSIS Act). Executive Order on the processing by the Danish Security and Intelligence Service (DSIS) of information about natural and legal persons, etc. (Executive Order No. 763 of 20 June 2014), as amended (most recently by Executive Order No. 438 of 7 April 2022) (the DSIS Executive Order). (As the latest amendment to the Executive Order did not come into force until 12 April 2022, it will not be discussed in detail in this annual report). Executive Order on security measures to protect personal information on natural and legal persons being processed by the Danish Security and Intelligence Service (DSIS) (Executive Order No. 516 of 23 May 2018 (the DSIS Executive Order on Security Measures). Decree No. 1622 of 17 November 2020 on the entry into force for Greenland of the Danish Security and Intelligence Service (DSIS) Act. Decree No. 1623 of 17 November 2020 on the entry into force for the Faroe Islands of the Danish Security and Intelligence Service (DSIS) Act. Act on the collection, use and storage of airline passenger name records (the PNR Act) (Act No. 1706 of 27 December 2018). Executive Order on the PNR Unit's processing of PNR information (Executive Order No. 1035 of 29 June 2020).[17]

Chapter 5

# Overview of France's Intelligence Legal Framework

## Félix Tréguer

*The Intelligence Act of 24 July 2015 (loi relative au renseignement) is a statute adopted by the French Parliament. The law created a new chapter in the Code of Internal Security aimed at regulating the surveillance programs of French intelligence agencies, in particular those of the DGSI (domestic intelligence) and the DGSE (foreign intelligence).*

## Background

The Intelligence Bill was introduced to the Parliament on 19 March 2015 by French Prime Minister Manuel Valls (Socialist Party) and presented as the government's reaction to the Charlie Hebdo shootings. Despite widespread mobilisation, the Bill was adopted with 438 votes in favour, 86 against and 42 abstentions at the National Assembly and 252 for, 67 against and 26 abstentions at the Senate. It was made into law on 24 July 2015. Although framed by the government as a response to the Paris attacks of January 2015, the passage of the Intelligence Act has a much longer history. The previous law providing a framework for the surveillance programs of French intelligence agencies was the Wiretapping Act of 1991, aimed at regulating telephone wiretaps. Many surveillance programs developed in the 2000s–especially to monitor Internet communications—were rolled out outside of any legal framework. As early as 2008, the French government's White Paper of Defence and National Security stressed that "intelligence activities do not have the benefit of a clear and sufficient legal framework," and said that "legislative adjustments" were necessary. A first and partial attempt at legalisation went underway right after the first

Snowden disclosures, with the adoption of the 2013 Military Planning Act in the fall of 20131. Since it was first adopted, the 2015 Intelligence Act has been amended several times, either in response to new case-law by French and supranational courts, in order to clarify specific provisions whose interpretations had led to controversies within the world of intelligence, and/or to expand intelligence agencies' capabilities. The most significant revision came about in July 20212.[2]

## General Provisions

Compared to the 1991 Wiretapping Act (the previous statute in the field of secret sate surveillance), the 2015 Intelligence Act enacts an unprecedented extension of the scope of so-called "intelligence-gathering techniques" (see below).

### *Purpose of Intelligence*

Article L. 811-3,[3] also extends the number of objectives that can justify extra-judicial surveillance. These include:

1. National independence, territorial integrity and national defence;

2. Major interests in foreign policy, implementation of European and international obligations of France and prevention of all forms of foreign interference;

3. Major economic, industrial and scientific interests of France;

4. Prevention of terrorism;

5. Prevention of: a) attacks on the republican nature of institutions; b) actions towards continuation or reconstitution of groups disbanded under Article L. 212-1; c) collective violence likely to cause serious harm to public peace;

6. Prevention of organised crime and delinquency;

7. Prevention of proliferation of weapons of mass destruction.

The government is allowed to extend by decree the number of law enforcement agencies who may conduct extra-judicial surveillance.[4] Finally, any telecom operator or hosting providers failing to comply with the data requests or other surveillance measures can be punished by a two-year imprisonment term and a €150,000 fine (article L. 881-2).

## Oversight

The existing oversight commission, the CNCIS (established in 1991), is replaced by a new Commission called the "National Oversight Commission for Intelligence-Gathering Techniques" (Commission Nationale de contrôle des techniques de renseignement, or CNCTR). According to the final version of the Intelligence Act –and much like the CNCIS it is comprised of nine members:

1. Four MPs designated by the Presidents of the Presidents of both chambers of Parliament[5]

2. Two administrative judges and two judicial judges designated respectively by the Council of State and the Cour de Cassation;

3. One technical expert designated by the telecom National Regulatory Authority (the addition of a commissioner with technical expertise was the main innovation).

The commissioners as well as their staff enjoy the highest security clearances so as to perform their duties. Against previous proposals of an oversight body with extended powers over intelligence agencies, the role of the CNCTR is restricted to the oversight of surveillance measures. The Commission has 24 hours to issue its ex ante non-binding opinion regarding the surveillance authorisations delivered by the Prime Minister before surveillance begins,6 except in cases of "absolute emergency" where it is simply notified of the surveillance measure within 24 hours upon deliverance (article L. 821-3). As for ex post oversight, the CNCTR is supposed to have "permanent, comprehensive and direct access to records, logs, collected intelligence, transcripts and extractions" of collected data. Six years after the adoption of the Act, the traceability of collected intelligence is reportedly insufficient. According to the DPR:

*"The main room for improvement today seems to lie in the still very uneven development, according to the services, of systems for tracing consultations, transcriptions and data extractions, which undeniably weighs on the CNCTR's capacity to conduct a complete and effective control."[7]*

The CNCTR is able to conduct visits, both planned and unforeseen, in the premises where these documents are centralised (article L. 833-2-2). If an irregularity is found, it can send to the Prime Minister a "recommendation" so that it can put an end to it. One hugely significant exception to the CNCTR's oversight powers are the bulk of data obtained or sent through data-sharing with foreign intelligence agencies (see below). Other bodies form part of the oversight structure for French intelligence:

1.  In the Fall of 2007, the government of President Nicolas Sarkozy introduced a bill establishing the "Parliamentary Delegation for Intelligence" (Délégation parlementaire au renseignement, or DPR), an eight-member strong bipartisan parliamentary committee charged with "keeping track (suivi) of the general activity and means" of intelligence agencies.[8] This was a tepid move, but nevertheless amounted to significant change: For the first time, the executive branch conceded to the legislative branch –which is structurally weak under the political regime of the Fifth Republic– some degree of first-hand knowledge of what was until then a "chasse gardée"[9].

2.  Inspired by the U.S. style of intelligence governance, several reforms also aimed at strengthening the "présidentialisation" of intelligence policy. In 2008, the Élysée created the office of National Intelligence Coordinator as well as the National Intelligence Council. At least on paper (because the President already had de facto authority on the DGSE), the reform undermined the Prime Minister's authority over intelligence agencies.

## "Intelligence-gathering techniques"

The Intelligence Act lists various procedures for the collection of communications intelligence.

### Wiretaps and access to metadata

Techniques of communications surveillance include telephone or Internet wiretaps (L. 852-1), surveillance of open WiFi networks (L. 852-2), the use of IMSI-Catchers (L. 851-6), satellite interceptions (L. 852-3), access to identifying data and other metadata (L. 851-1), geotagging (L. 851-4) and computer network exploitation (L. 853-2), all of which are subject to authorisation of a (renewable) duration of four months. The Acts also legalises the use of GPS-Tracking devices (L. 851-5) as well as covert listening devices in private premises (L.853-1).

### Automated and real-time analysis of metadata

The Act authorises the use of scanning devices (nicknamed "black boxes" by a government adviser in March 2015) to be installed on the infrastructures of telecom operators and hosting providers to analyse in real-time telephone or Internet metadata. Black boxes are authorised after an opinion by the CNCTR, for a duration of two months. Article L. 851-3 of the Code of Internal Security provides that: for the sole purpose of preventing terrorism, automated processing techniques may be imposed on the networks of [telecom operators and hosting providers] in order to detect, according to selectors specified in the authorisation, communications that are likely to reveal a terrorist threat.[10]

This provision led to much discussion during parliamentary debates. The Minister of Defence, Jean-Yves Le Drian, explained that the goal was to detect "connections at certain hours, from certain places, on certain websites." In that case, the operational goal is to detect the IP addresses or telephone numbers of known terrorist suspects with potential recruits, or to spot those who try to connect to a "terrorist website." The Director of the DGSE, Bernard Bajolet, gave another example during a committee hearing, asserting that the goal was to "discern clandestine attitudes," alluding to the use of cryptographic and anonymizing tools (for instance using a proxy server). As for the exact technical nature of these real-time traffic-scanning devices, critics of the proposal feared that the government would use potentially extremely intrusive technologies known as "Deep Packet Inspection" (DPI), which would enable the automatic analysis of all communications flowing through the network.[11] The government – this time through Interior Minister Bernard Cazeneuve, who complained about the "prevailing hubbub and media uproar"– said it would not use DPI. It took the government until 2017 to roll-out the first of these devices.

In mid-2021, when the sunset clause under which this provision was adopted finally came to end after being extended, the government submitted a report to the Parliament asserting that it had made a very limited use of the provision (according to the CNIL, the French data protection authority, only two or three of these black boxes have been deployed since 2017, and only for telephone metadata[12]). This limited use is apparently the consequence of a strong disagreement between the government and the CNCTR on the definition of metadata: whereas intelligence officials sought to scan URLs beyond mere domain names, the CNCTR opposed this move, citing constitutional case-law limiting the surveillance of communications content. To overcome this stalemate, the 2021 reform explicitly expanded the provision to cover detailed URLs. While the specifications were never made explicit in the 2021 reform bill, the government indicated to the CNCTR and to the CNIL that for technical reasons, rather than installing these black boxes on the infrastructure of technical intermediaries as it was the case since the 2015 reform, the later would be asked to copy their metadata traffic in bulk and send it to the Prime Minister's technical office task with implementing intelligence surveillance measures, the GIC (Groupement interministériel de contrôle), where it would be stored for 24 hours and scanned.[13] The CNIL expressed serious concerns and said that such an infrastructure of surveillance should be spelled out in the statute considering that it entailed an even more serious interference in the right to privacy. Even prior to these contentious changes, the provision appeared in breach of EU law. According to the La Quadrature du Net ruling of October 6th, 2020:

"the interference resulting from the automated analysis of traffic and location data, such as that at issue in the main proceedings, is particularly serious since it covers, generally and indiscriminately, the data of persons using electronic communication systems. That finding is all the more justified given that, as is clear from the national legislation at issue (...), the data that is the subject of the automated analysis is likely to reveal the nature of the information consulted online. In addition, such automated analysis is applied generally to all persons who use electronic communication systems and, consequently, applies also to persons with respect to whom there is no evidence capable of suggesting that their conduct might have a link, even an indirect or remote one, with terrorist activities."[14]

With this ruling, the Court indicated that this "particularly serious interference" could only meet the requirement of proportionality "only in situations in which a Member State is facing a serious threat to national security which is shown to be genuine and present or foreseeable, and provided that the duration of that retention is limited to what is strictly necessary." Finally, the Court stressed that the implementation of such automated surveillance of metadata must be "be subject to effective review, either by a court or by an independent administrative body whose decision is binding." Now, current French law does not seem to abide by any of these standards. Article L851-3 of the Internal Security Code authorises this measure in a general way and as a matter of principle, without being conditioned to any "genuine and present" threat (in its ruling of April 21st, 2021, the Council of State chose to shelter French law from the CJEU ruling by alleging that France was under a near-perpetual threat against its national security.[15] French law does not provide a framework for this measure within a "strictly limited period" and in practice these devices have been authorised without interruption for the past four years.

Lastly, authorisations to engage in such automated and real-time surveillance are subject to an ex ante opinion of the CNCTR, which by law is not binding (according to the CNCTR however, its opinions have never disregarded by the Government since the adoption of the Intelligence Act in 2015). Another provision limited to anti-terrorism allows for the real-time collection of metadata (article L. 851-3, for terrorism only and for a 4 months period). Initially, the provision targeted only individuals "identified as a [terrorist] threat." After the 2016 Nice Attack, it was extended by a Bill of the state of emergency to cover individuals "likely to be related to a threat" or who simply belong to "the entourage" of individuals "likely related to a threat". According to La Quadrature du Net, this means that the provision can now potentially cover "hundreds or even thousands of persons (...) rather than just the 11 700 individuals" reported to be on the French terrorism watch list." Following a decision by the Constitutional Council in response to a legal challenge introduced by La Quadrature du Net[16], a quota similar to those already in place for wiretaps was introduced to cap the maximum number of authorisations that can be valid at any given time (with a maximum of 720 simultaneous authorisations as of 2020).

## Computer Network Exploitation

The Act authorises hacking as a method for intelligence gathering. Article L. 853-2 allows for:

1. Access, collection, retention and transmission of computer data stored in a computer system;

2. Access, collection, retention and transmission of computer data, as it is displayed on a user's computer screen, as it is entered by keystrokes, or as received and transmitted by audio-visual peripheral devices. Considering the intrusiveness of computer hacking, the law provides that these techniques are authorised for a duration of thirty days, and only "when intelligence cannot be collected by any other legally authorised means." The data thus obtained can be stored for up to two months after collection.[17] The Act also grants blanket immunity to intelligence officers who carry on computer crimes into computer systems located abroad (article 323-8 of the Penal Code). This, in turn, may contravene article 32(b) of the Budapest Convention on Cybercrime on the transborder access to computer data.[18]

## Forced cooperation of private actors for bulk hacking

Although neither the explanatory memorandum nor the impact assessment carried out by the government mentioned it, article 12 of the 2021 reform made a few changes to the provisions listing the obligations of telecom operators. These changes were nevertheless addressed by Gérald Darmanin, minister of the Interior, when he explained on public radio that in order to circumvent the encryption of communications, "we are discussing with the major Internet companies, we are asking them to let us in via security holes, some accept it, and others do not. We probably need a law to constrain foreign services, it is coming."[19] Article 12, which amended article L. 871-6 of the Code of Internal Security, seems to allow intelligence agencies to compel operators and providers of electronic communications (such as Orange, SFR, but also WhatsApp or Signal according to EU law) to assist in the deployment of vulnerabilities on the terminals of targeted persons. This interpretation was confirmed by one of the bill's rapporteurs, and during subsequent Parliamentary debates. The Interior Minister then answered a question by a minority member of Parliament on the issue:

"As for encrypted messengers, such as Telegram, WhatsApp or Signal, they have precisely built their economic model on the guarantee of not being able to be listened to. Let's be clear: it's not about listening in on phone conversations that take place on these applications, but about taking advantage of the fact that they pass through internet connections. For the most dangerous targets, and under the control of the CNCTR, the collection of computer data will allow access to the computer terminal of the person who uses these messaging systems to collect the data that are stored in these messaging systems".

To illustrate this point, the minister explicitly referred to the Encrochat operation conducted in 2020, in which the French police deployed a particularly complex computer attack involving the exploitation of vulnerabilities to get access to hack the devices of thousands of phones at the same time.[20]

### Foreign surveillance

The Act also legalises the DGSE's bulk surveillance apparatus developed since 2008 under a chapter on the "surveillance of international communications." International communications are defined as "communications emitted from or received abroad," that is to say, to put it more simply, going in or out of the country. The legal regime created here is a complex one:

1. For the collection of "international communications," the Prime Minister "designates" (rather than "authorises") which network infrastructure (e.g. the cable-landing stations owned by telecom operators) are subject to large-scale interception (article L. 854-2-I).

2. After collection, "when it appears" that both ends of the communications are coming from "technical identifiers that are traceable to the national territory" (e.g.: emitter and receiver are using French telephone numbers or IP addresses), article L. 854-1 provides that intercepted communications "shall be immediately deleted," unless the persons targeted are physically located abroad and either i) already covered by a national surveillance authorisation or are ii) deemed to be a national security threat. However, given the transnational nature of Internet communications, and the fact that a communication between two French residents is likely to be routed in and out of French borders, one can doubt on the effectiveness of such a safeguard.

3. For bulk analysis of intercepted metadata (what the Act calls "non individualised exploitation" of metadata), the Prime Minister issues an one-year authorisation specifying the purposes of such analysis and which intelligence agencies are in charge of conducting it (article L.854-2-II). This seems to refer to the automated-scanning of intercepted metadata, similar to black boxes, but this time not restricted to anti-terrorism.

4. For the exploitation of the content of communications or of their metadata, the Prime Minister issues a four-month authorisation specifying the purposes justifying such analysis, the intelligence agencies in charge, as well as targeted geographic zones, organisations, groups of people or individuals.

Originally, the CNCTR was only notified of all authorisations related to international surveillance and can issue recommendations to the Prime Minister if irregularities were found. However, a few months after the adoption of the 2015 Intelligence Act and at the request of the Prime Minister, the CNCTR agreed to conduct such ex ante oversight on an experimental basis by issuing prior opinions over requests for the exploitation of intercepted communications provided for in section III of Article L. 854-2. This extension of the CNCTR's oversight powers has been effective since the end of May 2016. In 2018, the law was amended to provide a legal basis for this ex ante oversight.[21] In breach of European law, French law does not provide any redress mechanisms for foreigners (including people living in other EU Member States) that might be subject to international surveillance measures.

## Data retention periods

For national surveillance measures, once communications data are collected by intelligence agencies, retention periods are the following:

1. Content (correspondences): 1 month after collection (for encrypted content, period starts after decryption, within the limit of 6 years after initial collection);

2. Metadata: 4 years (compared to the LPM decree 3-year period).

For international surveillance, retention periods depend on whether one end of the communication uses a "technical identifiers traceable to the national territory" or not, in which case the "national" retention periods are applicable, but they start after the first exploitation and no later than six months after collection (article L. 854-8). If both ends of the communication are foreign, the following periods apply:

1. Content: 1 year after first exploitation, within the limit of 4 years after collection (for encrypted content, periods starts after decryption, within the limit of 8 years after collection);

2. Metadata: 6 years.

## Data-sharing between French intelligence agencies

The 2018 reform amended the provisions regarding international surveillance in order to facilitate the use of DGSE's data by domestic intelligence for French residents – surveillance activities that the original 2015 Act had sought to restrict[22]. As Florence Parley, then Minister of Armed Forces, explained upon introducing the amendment; "First, we want to allow the exploitation of data of a technical identifier traceable to the national territory intercepted in the context of the surveillance of international communications, even though its user is in France." Article L. 854-2 V thus provides a new type of surveillance technique, where the Prime Minister allows – after an opinion by the CNCTR – for the exploitation of the content of communications and/or metadata collected through international surveillance of a person currently in France – something that the 2015 Intelligence Act had explicitly ruled out. The same provision also provides for wiretaps and metadata surveillance authorisations issued in the context of domestic intelligence (articles L. 851-1,L. 851-2 and L. 852-1 I) can also encompass the exploitation of data collected and stored under the international surveillance regime. Secondly, the government sought to authorise surveillance operations known as "doubt removal". According to the minister of Armed Forces:

"The removal of doubt will take the form of a spot check on metadata legally intercepted in the context of international communications surveillance. These are very quick operations, ones that are not repeated and are likely to reveal a relationship graph or the presence of a person abroad, who could then be monitored if he or she presents a threat. As soon as the verification reveals the need for surveillance, the exploitation of communications can only be pursued via the intelligence techniques enshrined in the 2015 law."[23] Through this new provision, intelligence analysts are able to use one or more "selectors" or "identifiers" corresponding to persons or groups of persons located abroad to probe databases for French-related metadata. By doing so, they can build the target's social graph and identify other potential suspects currently in France. These suspects' communications can then be further monitored under the national surveillance regime (e.g., by requesting authorisation to conduct a security interception). In the case of a "urgent" terrorist threat or national cybersecurity threat, "doubt removal" queries can exceptionally be conducted with French technical identifiers and cover not only metadata but also the content of communication.

In such case, it becomes possible to retrace the history of a French resident's communications by going back six years in the past (data retention period provided for in the "international surveillance" regime), whereas the national surveillance regime allowed for the collection of metadata from operators and a number of hosting companies that were no more than one year old. Beyond the special case of international surveillance and the use of data collected under this regime by domestic intelligence, French intelligence agencies can share data and intelligence. The original drafting of the 2015 Intelligence Act did not provide any strong safeguards for such data sharing, as the government declined for years to adopt an implementation decree.

In April 2019, Le Monde revealed that a data warehouse (an infrastructure nicknamed "entrepôt") had been built next to the DGSE facilities to provide a kind of "fusion center" to French intelligence agencies.[24] Finally, with the threat of litigation rising, the 2021 reform bill established a more detailed legal regime for these activities. Article L. 822-3 now provides that collected data and associated intelligence can be shared with other agencies. Such data sharing is subject to an authorisation of the Prime Minister and a prior opinion of the CNCTR if i) the data is shared for different purposes than those that justified the original authorisation (e.g. ancillary use of data for counter-espionage purposes when the data was first collected for the purpose of fighting terrorism) or ii) when the intelligence agency with which the data is shared has no prerogative over the matter for which collection was first authorised. Lastly, article L. 863-2 of the Code of Internal Security provides that intelligence services may require any data, including personal data (with the exception of genetic data) to other public bodies.

### *Experimentation and Research*

In 2018, the French government built on a provision first adopted in 2017 to expand the possibility for agencies part of the Ministry of the Armed Forces to engage in trials of surveillance devices like IMSI catchers or those used for international surveillance and the surveillance of radio communications (article 2371-2 of the Code of Defence). The CNCTR is notified prior to the roll-out of these tests and is informed of their scope. In 2021, the government introduced another legislative provision dedicated to research and development. Next to the DGSE's Big Data tools, French domestic intelligence has also worked with Palantir's technologies from 2016 onwards to mine and analyse collected data[25]. The growing use of Artificial Intelligence techniques led to the adoption of article L. 822-2 III, which provides that collected data can be stored for up to five years and used as training data for "the acquisition of sufficient knowledge to develop, improve and validate the technical capacities of collection and exploitation."

## Redress Mechanism

The Intelligence Act reorganises redress procedures against secret surveillance, establishing – and this is one of the main innovations of the 2015 Act–the possibility to introduce a legal challenge before the Council of State. The procedure is the following:

1.  Any legal person can introduce a complaint to the CNCTR, asking the oversight body to investigate whether or not she has been subject to illegal surveillance measures (article L. 833-4). The CNCTR can then only notify the plaintiff it has carried out necessary checks, "without confirming or denying" whether or not they have been spied upon.

2.  Only after taking this preliminary step, plaintiffs can appeal to the Council of State, who is competent in first and last resort. The same procedure is opened to the CNCTR when its investigations uncover irregularities but only when, once notified by the CNCTR, the Prime Minister has failed to take appropriate action.

3.  Intelligence-related cases are adjudicated by a new, three-judge special court within the Council of State (so-called "specialised panel"or "specialised court"). The court's judges and their staff have security clearance and can access any piece of information collected by the CNCTR (initial authorisation, collected transcripts, etc.). The Act provides that the right of the defense, and in particular the right to open justice, may be "accommodated" to protect classified information. In practice, much of the evidence presented by the government to justify the necessity and proportionality of the surveillance measure will remain hindered from the plaintiffs and her lawyers (article L. 773-2 of the Code of Administrative Justice).

4.  When it finds a surveillance operation to be illegal, the specialised court can (but is not obliged to) put an end to it and/or order the collected data to be destroyed (article L. 773-7 of the Code of Administrative Justice). Without compromising state secrets, it can then inform the plaintiff that the government has carried out an illegal act, and order the state to pay damages.

This redress procedure seems inspired by the so-called "closed-material procedure" established in the UK through the Justice and Security Act of 2013, which are criticised for their detrimental impact on defence rights.[26]The DPR has also stressed the shortcomings of this redress mechanism: "The specialised panel appears unable to ensure, if this were to be raised in the context of litigation, that the intelligence techniques used do not lead to the collection of data other than that for which they were authorised, or that the database relating to state security comply, in their operation and content, with the legal framework and fundamental freedoms. The president of the specialised panel of the Council of State also observed that lawmakers had not adopted any specific provision to guarantee the implementation, by the intelligence agencies, of its rulings regarding intelligence techniques."[27]

## Major oversight gaps in the French intelligence legal framework

In this last section, we provide an overview of some major oversight gaps in the French legal framework surrounding intelligence.

## International data-sharing

Article L. 833-2-3 explicitly forbids the CNCTR to conduct any form of oversight on data shared with foreign intelligence partners. Following criticisms by civil society organisations during the parliamentary debate in 2015 the CNCTR has voiced in several annual reports an important oversight gap regarding the sharing of data between French intelligence services and foreign services. In France, the issue is all the more pressing because the data flows exchanged between the General Directorate for External Security (DGSE) and the National Security Agency (NSA) have increased rapidly following the conclusion of the SPINS agreements, signed at the end of 2015 between France and the United States[28].Yet the 2015 law explicitly excluded any control by the CNCTR over these international collaborations nurtured by networks of intelligence professionals enjoying strong autonomy. In its annual report published in 2019[29],the CNCTR admitted that this "black hole" in intelligence control presented a major risk, since it could allow French services to receive data from their counterparts that they would not have been able to obtain legally through the procedures provided by French law. The CNCTR considered that "a reflection [should] be carried out on the legal framework for data exchanges between French intelligence services and their foreign partners." In support of this request, the CNCTR referred to the case law of the European Court of Human Rights (ECHR), which again recalled in its Big Brother Watch v. United Kingdom judgment of May 25, 2021 that these exchanges should be governed by national law and subject to the control of an independent authority[30]. According to a report by the Fundamental Rights Agency of the EU, France is currently the last European Union member state to have no legal framework for these international exchanges.[31]

## Right to information of persons under surveillance

Another essential principle identified by European case law is the right to information of persons who have been the subject of a surveillance measure, once such information is no longer likely to hinder the investigation conducted against them by intelligence agencies. In a report published in January 2018, the CNCTR reviewed the relevant case law and mentioned several examples of foreign legislation – German law in particular– guaranteeing a procedure for notifying persons under surveillance and providing for a number of narrowly limited exceptions. The CNCTR was forced to note that, as French law stands, "persons under surveillance cannot be informed of the intelligence techniques implemented against them."32 The 2021 reform bill completely overlooked this issue. The government has also set aside another requirement, again stressed by the Council of State in its ruling of April 21, 2021 on the indiscriminate retention of metadata. In this decision, which largely won the government's case, the Conseil d'État echoed the CJEU's La Quadrature du Net's ruling by indicating that the opinions rendered by the CNCTR on surveillance measures should be "binding" rather than merely consultative. In spite of the CNIL's insistence that the 2021 reform bill should address this concern, the government refused to do so.

### Lack of oversight on intelligence databases

As for the joint desire of the DPR and the CNCTR to guarantee the latter a right of review over intelligence databases, it is coming up against the fierce opposition of the services. As parliamentarians from the DPR have emphasised, this is a crucial stage in the oversight process, as it is the only way for the CNCTR to "ensure that no data has been collected, transcribed or extracted in disregard of the legal framework, or even in the absence of an authorisation granted by the Prime Minister."[33] And yet, a person close to the Ministry of the Interior complains about the regulatory burdens. According to them, "the police are required to do crazy things" and "even the smallest pizza vendor can cross-reference more computer data than our intelligence agencies."[34]

### No legal framework for OSINT, infiltration and postal surveillance

The French legal framework around intelligence is completely silent regarding other typical surveillance techniques that are extremely sensitive from the point of view of civil liberties. This is the case of the surveillance of letters and postal packages, or the infiltration of certain groups by intelligence agents. In the United Kingdom, however, the Investigatory Powers Act of 2016 covers these two areas. The French law also makes no mention of so-called "open source" surveillance, notably on social networks such as Facebook or Twitter–an activity about which little has been leaked to the press but which is known to have grown in importance over the last ten years.[35] The DPR recently confirmed it was the case: "[French] intelligence agencies collect and exploit intelligence of cyber origin from the innumerable sources freely available on the Internet, but also by means of techniques which are subject to a legal framework (. . . )."[36] Still, a high-ranking intelligence officials was quoted by a journalist as complaining over the bureaucratic burdens entailed by French law, claiming that "we have the most restrictive regulations in Europe: we have to constantly ask for authorisations from the CNCTR."[37]

## *Right to information and whistleblowing*

Apart from the few pieces of information that have filtered through thanks to the small circle of specialised journalists who have access to sources within the services, and apart from the rare allusions made concerning these topics by those in charge of intelligence during parliamentary hearings or by the CNCTR, no official information is provided on the nature of the technologies used by the services and their imbrication in the processes of production of intelligence, on the public contracts and the identity of the private subcontractors, nor even on the legal interpretations that are used within the services. Here again, the comparison with the main European intelligence powers reveals the French democratic delay. To be convinced of this, one simply has to consult the report published in August 2016 by David Anderson in the margin of the parliamentary debate on the Investigatory Powers Act.[38] This jurist in charge of the independent monitoring of anti-terrorism legislation reported on the technological capacities for "bulk powers" data collection and exploitation.

He also gave several examples of use cases in which these technologies were employed and evaluated their operational interest based on internal documents and interviews with certain senior officials. In France, such a degree of transparency seems unimaginable for the moment. Even if the CNCTR has made some progress in the precision of the information provided in its reports, it is essentially content to describe the state of the law and its evolution, or to disseminate general statistics on the types of measures authorised and their purposes. This is still far from the level of detail that feeds the public debate and the work of parliamentarians, journalists or NGOs in countries such as the United Kingdom or Germany. Finally, following a recommendation of the Council of State in its 2014 report, Urvoas, the 2015 Intelligence Bill rapporteur at the National Assembly, passed an amendment turning the CNCTR into an internal whistle-blowing channel for intelligence officers. But the provision remains very limited in scope.[39]Moreover, the Act increases the criminal repression of disclosures regarding the "existence of the deployment" of a given surveillance technique (article L. 881-1): Such unauthorised disclosures are punished by a two year imprisonment term and a €150 000 fine (against a two-year term and a €30 000 fine before). Lastly, the court rulings of the Council of State's special section and its general case-law will remain secret (article L. 773-7 of the Code of Administrative Justice). All of these provisions affecting the right to information obviously fail to comply with international best-practices, such as those laid down in the Tshwane principles on national security and the right to information.[40]

and a schedule of upcoming events, all related to the four components of the plan and covering all scientific disciplines. Also, more specifically it features: the work produced by the CoSo's permanent colleges, expert groups and the Committee's various projects; an 'initiation' page for Internet users who want to find out more about Open Science; an 'Open Science Stories' page which highlights researchers implementing Open Science practices. You can also consult our Open Science newsletters (only available in French) and sign up to receive them. The Open Science movement aims to build an ecosystem in which science will be more cumulative, more supported by data, more transparent, faster and will provide universal access. Open Science is the free dissemination of the results, methods and products of scientific research. It is based on the opportunity the digital transformation represents to help develop open access to publications and – as far as possible – to data, source codes and research methods. There are several ways of disseminating open access publications. For example, self-archiving scientific productions in an open archive (sometimes called green open access) or publishing in an open access journal with or without APCs (sometimes called gold open access). Personal data–Data concerning an individual who is identified or identifiable. Green route–The green route refers to self-archiving by researchers or archiving by a third party of articles in open archives. The availability of an article may be delayed if an embargo is attached to it. Gold route–A journal is "gold" if all its articles are freely and immediately available on the journal's website, regardless of how it is funded. Félix Tréguer. Overview of France's Intelligence Legal Framework. [Research Report] Centre de recherches internationales (CERI). 2021, 19 p. halshs-01399548v2. December 2021. *Félix Tréguer is associate researcher at the CNRS Center for Internet and Society and postdoctoral fellow at CERI-Sciences Po. His research blends political history and theory, law as well as media and technology studies to look at the political history of the Internet and computing, power practices like surveillance and censorship, the algorithmic governmentality of the public sphere, and more broadly the digital transformation of the state and of the security field. He is a founding member of La Quadrature du Net, a French advocacy group dedicated to the defence of civil rights in relation to digital technologies. Contact: felix.treguer@sciencespo.fr – CERI 56 rue Jacob – 75006 Paris FRANCE. Acknowledgement: This research was supported by the French National Research Agency (ANR) through the GUARDINT project (Grant n°18-ORAR-0006-01). felix.treguer@sciencespo.fr.

Chapter 6

# Intelligence Reform and the Snowden Paradox: The Case of France

*Félix Tréguer*

## Abstract

Taking France as a case study, this article reflects on the ongoing legalisation strategies pursued by liberal states as they seek to secure and expand the Internet surveillance programs of their domestic and foreign intelligence agencies. Following the path to legalisation prior to and after the Snowden disclosures of 2013, the article shows how post-Snowden controversies helped mobilise advocacy groups against the extra judicial surveillance of Internet communications, a policy area which had hitherto been overlooked by French human rights groups. It also points to the dilemma that post-Snowden contention created for governments. On the one hand, the disclosures helped document the growing gap between the existing legal framework and actual surveillance practices, exposing them to litigation and thereby reinforcing the rationale for legalisation. On the other hand, they made such a legislative reform politically risky and unpredictable. In France, policy-makers navigated these constraints through a cautious mix of silence, denials, and securitisation. After the Paris attacks of January 2015 and a hasty deliberation in Parliament, the Intelligence Act was passed, making it the most extensive piece of legislation ever adopted in France to regulate secret state surveillance. The article concludes by pointing to the paradoxical effect of post-Snowden contention: French law now provides for clear rules authorising large-scale surveillance, to a degree of detail that was hard to imagine just a few years ago.

## Introduction

In January 2008, a meeting took place in the office of then President of France, Nicolas Sarkozy, at the Élysée Palace. In front of him sat Prime Minister François Fillon and the Director of the Direction Générale de la Sécurité Extérieure (DGSE, France's foreign intelligence agency) Pierre Brochand, as well as a few of their staff. Brochand had come with a plea. France, he explained, was on the verge of losing the Internet surveillance arms race. From the 1980's on, French intelligence services had managed to develop top-notch communications intelligence (COMINT) capabilities, thanks to a network of intercept stations located across metropolitan France and overseas territories, sometimes in partnership with the German Bundesnachrichtendienst, or BND. But as almost all of the world's communications were now travelling on IP based networks, the DGSE was losing ground on its main partners and competitors—in particular, the National Security Agency (NSA) and the British Government Communications Headquarters (GCHQ) France had some serious catching up to do, but it also had important assets.

First, its geographic location, with almost two dozen submarine cables landing on its shores, both in Brittany, Normandy and the Marseilles area. Second, its engineering elite state schools and high tech firms—not least of which submarine cable operators Alcatel and Orange as well as surveillance technology provider Qosmos—, which could provide the technical know-how necessary to carry on this ambitious project. Sarkozy was hesitant at first. The plan was very costly and its legality more than dubious. The French legal basis for communications surveillance dated back to 1991. Another issue was that of cost. At the time, the 2008 financial crisis had yet to unleash, but the government was already facing recurring deficits and it needed to contain public spending.

But Pierre Brochand and its supporters in the President's staff turned out to be convincing. Sarkozy eventually agreed to move forward with the proposed plan: Over the course of the next five years, the DGSE would get the €700 million it needed to upgrade its surveillance capabilities and hire over 600 staff to work in its Technical Directorate (the number of DGSE employees was then 4,440). Only six months later, near Marseilles, the first of the new intercept stations was up and running, doubling up the traffic coming from international cables, filtering it and transmitting it to the DGSE's headquarters in Paris. How do we even know about this meeting? We owe this account to journalist Vincent Jauvert, who revealed its existence in a French weekly magazine on July 1st 2015, at the very end of the parliamentary debate on the 2015 Intelligence Bill (Jauvert, 2015). According to former high ranking officials quoted by Jauvert, these efforts paid off: "When we turned on the faucet, it was a shock! All this information, it was unbelievable!" All of sudden, France was back in the game. To such an extent that, a few months later, in 2009, the NSA even offered to make the DGSE a member of the exclusive Five Eyes club.

Apparently, the "Sixth Eye" deal failed over the Central Intelligence Agency's (CIA) refusal to conclude a nospy agreement with France, and in 2011, a more modest cooperation was eventually signed between the NSA and the DGSE under the form of a memorandum—most likely the so-called LUSTRE agreement revealed in 2013 by NSA whistleblower Edward Snowden (Follorou, 2013). Another agreement was struck in November 2010 with the British GCHQ. Jauvert's report connected many pieces of information of what was—and still remains—a puzzle. By then, a few public statements by intelligence officials had already hinted at the formidable growth of the DGSE's Internet surveillance capabilities. The Snowden documents and a handful of investigative reports had also given evidence of France's rank in the world of COMINT.

However, for the first time, we were able to get a sense of some of the political intricacies and secret negotiations that presided over the rise of the most significant Internet surveillance program developed by French agencies, as well as their geopolitical outcomes. But his report also raised questions: If the plan agreed upon at the Élysée Palace in January 2008 was so successful, why did the new French administration wait until the Spring of 2015 to "go public" by presenting the Intelligence Bill aimed at legalising this large-scale surveillance program?

The goal of this paper—adapted from a longer research report (Tréguer, 2016a)—is to study the process of legalisation of Internet surveillance capabilities, taking France as a case study to analyse the impact of post-Snowden contention on the techno-legal apparatus of surveillance, one that has become deeply embedded in the daily routine of security professionals in domestic and transnational security fields. To provide an empirical analysis of this process of legalisation, the article uses the methodological toolbox of contentious politics, a sub-field of political sociology (Tilly & Tarrow, 2015). It first looks at historical antecedents of legalisation and contention around communications surveillance in France.

By providing a content analysis of recent investigative reports and policy documents to shed light on a policy domain veiled in secrecy, the paper points to the growing gap between secret surveillance practices and the law prior to the Snowden disclosures of 2013. It then turns to the impact of these leaks and the resulting episodes of contention for the strengthening of privacy advocacy in France, its chilling effect on legalisation, as well as the role of the terrorist threat and associated processes of securitisation in the adoption of the Intelligence Act of 2015. While calling for cross-country comparisons of intelligence reforms passed by liberal regimes since 2013, this case study concludes by suggesting that, rather than helping restore the rule of law, post-Snowden contention might paradoxically contribute to reinforcing illiberal trends towards the circumvention of procedural and substantive human rights safeguards, while strengthening the executive power's ability to "rule by law" (Tarrow, 2015, p. 162).

## Before Snowden, Legalisation Was Underway

As many of its counterparts, France has a record of surveillance scandals. In 1974, a project by the Interior Ministry—aimed at building a huge database gathering as much information as possible on its citizens—sparked a huge outcry, after an unidentified engineer working on the project blew the whistle by speaking to the press (Joinet, 2013). The "SAFARI affair", named after the codename of the project, played an important role in the adoption of the French personal data protection framework in 1978 (Fuster, 2014).

### The Wiretapping Act of 1991: An Antecedent of Legalisation

In 1991, following two condemnations by the European Court of Human Rights (ECHR) pointing to the lack of detailed provision surrounding both judicial and administrative wiretaps, the government rushed to Parliament to pass the Wiretapping Act, which provided the first comprehensive legal framework regulating the surveillance of telephone communications (Errera, 2003). In the early 1990's, the prospect of Internet surveillance was of course still very distant, and the law was drafted with landline and wireless (satellite in particular) telephone communications in mind. So when tapping into Internet traffic became an operational necessity for intelligence agencies at the end of the 1990's, its legal basis was progressively hinged on secret and extensive interpretations of existing provisions (one notable exception was a 2006 statute which authorised administrative access to metadata records for the sole purpose of anti-terrorism) (Tréguer, 2016b).

Such was the case of the DGSE's large-scale Internet surveillance programme launched in 2008, and apparently backed by a provision of the 1991 Wiretapping Act that gave a blank check to the DGSE to conduct bulk interceptions of so-called "Hertzian transmissions" without any oversight. French officials looking back at these developments have often resorted to euphemisms, talking about a zone of "a-legality" to describe this secret creep in surveillance capabilities (e.g. Follorou & Johannès, 2013). Although "a-legality" may be used to characterise the legal grey areas in which citizens operate to exert and claim new rights that have yet to be sanctioned by either the parliament or the courts—for instance the disclosure of huge swathes of digital documents (Tréguer, 2015)—it cannot adequately qualify these instances of legal tinkering by secret bureaucracies that seek to escape the safeguards associated with the rule of law. Indeed, when the state interferes with civil rights like privacy and freedom of communication, a detailed, public and proportionate legal basis authorising them to do so is required by supranational courts like the ECHR. Otherwise, such interferences are, quite plainly, illegal.

### Legal Insecurity as a Driver for Legalisation

Secret legal interpretations are, of course, a common feature in the field of surveillance (Rubinstein, Nojeim, & Lee, 2014), and the extralegal regulation of Internet communications has become increasingly common among liberal regimes (Benkler, 2011; Tréguer, 2015). In France, as we will see, they could prosper all the more easily given the shortcomings of human rights advocacy against Internet surveillance. But even so, French national security policy-makers began to worry that the existing framework failed to comply with the standards of the ECHR. In July 2008, six months after the launch of the DGSE's large-scale Internet surveillance program, the government released the White Paper of Defence and National Security—a major effort of strategic planning conducted under Sarkozy's presidency. This official policy document claimed, for what appears to be the first time that intelligence legislation would soon be presented to Parliament:" Intelligence activities do not have the benefit of a clear and sufficient legal framework. This shortcoming must be corrected. A new legal architecture will define the duties of intelligence agencies, safeguards for both their personnel and human sources, as well as overarching rules for the protection of classified information. Legislative amendments will be provided, while respecting the balance between the protection of civil rights, the effectiveness of judicial proceedings and the protection of secrecy. (French Government, 2008, p. 142)

The document added that "the consultation of metadata and administrative databases...will be enlarged". But the following September, a major scandal erupted around the adoption of a decree authorising a very broad intelligence database—named EDVIGE—for domestic surveillance purposes. Within a few weeks, a widespread civil society mobilisation against the decree led the government to backtrack (Marzouki, 2009). It marked one of the biggest episodes of human rights contention under Sarkozy's presidency and was apparently enough to put the government's broader plans for modernising intelligence law to rest until the end of its mandate. What a conservative, "tough-on-security" government could not achieve would eventually be pursued and carried out by a left-of-center, supposedly pro civil rights party. By the time the Socialist Party returned to power in 2012, its officials in charge of security affairs were the ones pushing for a sweeping reform that would legally secure the work of people in the intelligence community and, incidentally, put France in line with democratic standards (which require a public and detailed legal basis for the surveillance activities of intelligence agencies).

One man played an important role in this process: Jean-Jacques Urvoas, a long-time proponent of intelligence reform in the Socialist Party, who became Minister of Justice in early 2016. After the 2012 elections, Urvoas was re-elected to the National Assembly and awarded with the prestigious position of President of the Committee on Legal Affairs. This also made him a de facto member of the Parliament's Committee on Intelligence, sealing his membership to the small circle of intelligence policymakers. Mid-May 2013—just two weeks before the first Guardian article based on the Snowden files—, Urvoas presented a 200-page-long bipartisan report on the "evolution of the legal framework of intelligence services" (Urvoas & Verchère, 2013). In one section entitled "Tomorrow, a Condemnation by the ECHR?", the report provided an overview of the court's case law and insisted that: In France, for lack of legislation adapted to certain aspects of their activities, intelligence services are forced to act outside of any legal framework.... The interception of communication, the listening of places and the tapping of images violate the right to private life, as do the geo-localisation of a phone or of a vehicle.... Concretely, France is risking a condemnation by the European Court of Human Rights for violating the European Convention on Human Rights. For the time being, no legal challenge has been introduced against intelligence-related activities, but there is a constant risk of condemnation. (p. 31) Recalling the ECHR 1990 rulings against France, the section ended with an invitation to engage in an intelligence reform based on a careful analysis of the ECHR case law in the field of secret surveillance. But despite this acknowledgement that intelligence agencies had been engaging in illegal surveillance, there was no reaction from human rights groups.

## After Snowden, Legalisation Sparked Contention

While the global anti-surveillance contention unleashed by Snowden reinforced intelligence policy-makers' rationale for legalisation by documenting surveillance practices to litigation, it also made such reform more exposed to public scrutiny and therefore politically riskier. However, probably comforted by the fact that French privacy advocates had traditionally overlooked the issue of Internet surveillance, policy-makers nevertheless gave it a try. In late 2013, a first attempt at partial legalisation was introduced, eventually giving rise to new alliances among advocacy groups.

### Initial (Lack of) Contention

Initially, the reaction of the French civil society to the Snowden disclosures—the first of which appeared in a Guardian article on June 5th 2013—was relatively mild. Like in the US, the UK, Germany, and other countries, there was of course widespread media coverage of the Snowden affair in June, July and August of that year. Many French Non-Governmental Organisations (NGOs) active in the field of human rights joined the media frenzy. Some international organisations with presence in France, like Amnesty or Human Rights Watch, were able to get traction from the initiatives launched elsewhere, occupying the French public sphere by translating press releases targeting the US and the UK agencies.

Digital rights organisations working on the overhaul of the EU framework for data protection, like La Quadrature du Net (LQDN), mentioned Snowden in passing in their public communications on the matter, but because they were busy working on the proposed EU regulation on data protection, they targeted the data collection practices of Internet firms rather than state surveillance (LQDN, 2013). The only notable exception to this relative apathy was the Fédération Internationale des Droits de l'Homme (FIDH), the worldwide movement for human rights founded in 1922, which filed a criminal complaint against NSA's PRISM program and appealed to the UN Special Rapporteur for Freedom of Expression, calling for an investigation into the facts revealed by Snowden (FIDH, 2013). However, despite the recent Urvoas report hinting at the discrepancy between surveillance practices of French agencies and the law, none of these groups sought to turn the Snowden scandal into an opportunity to call, say, for an independent review of the DGSE's capabilities, or bring new privacy safeguards to a legal framework that was visibly outdated. How can we explain such lack of substantive contention?

## Denials as Legitimisation Strategies

For one, even in activist circles, there was a feeling that the whole affair was mostly related to the NSA and the GCHQ, not to French agencies. In this regard, the legitimation strategies of policy-makers, which denied that French agencies were engaging in the same practices as their Five Eyes counterparts—a strategy also observed in Germany (Schulze, 2015)—, were successful. But even more than denials, it was a no-comment policy that dominated the French government's response to the unfolding scandal. One notable exception to this wall of communication was Urvoas. On June 12th, in Le Monde, the then member of Parliament refuted that French agencies were conducting large-scale surveillance of Internet communications, claiming: "I have never heard of tools that could be associated to what the Americans use, and every time I asked intelligence officials, I got a negative answer". (Chapuis, 2013). But two weeks later, on July 4th, Le Monde ran a piece by reporter Jacques Follorou on the "French Big Brother", claiming that France was "doing the same thing" as the NSA: "Le Monde is able to reveal the General Directorate for External Security (DGSE, special services) systematically collects electromagnetic signals coming from computers or telephones in France, as well as traffic between French and foreigners: the totality of our communications is being spied upon. All emails, SMS, telephone records, connections to Facebook, Twitter, are then stored for years". (Follorou & Johannès, 2013)

The report also quoted a high-ranking intelligence official arguing that these practices were "a legal" (i.e. in a legal grey area) rather than illegal (for lack of any public and detailed legal basis). Considering what we now know about the DGSE's Internet surveillance programs and given also the provision of the 1991 Wiretapping Act allowing bulk collection of wireless communications, the article could have triggered a new scandal, directly aimed at French agencies. But because its sensationalist tone and several inaccuracies—most importantly the fact that it was technically infeasible for the DGSE to collect the "totality" of French communications—, it appeared overblown and was easily dismissed. Once again, Urvoas was one of the only officials to comment. He immediately published a blog post refuting these allegations, using what would become a favoured metaphor in intelligence circles to distinguish French agencies from the NSA: "In comparison to the NSA, a technical agency dedicated only to interceptions, the DGSE is a non-specialised agency collecting intelligence for the sole purpose of complying with its regulatory duties. We could thus say that, against the 'fishing trawls' that the NSA seems to be operating, the DGSE is conducting "harpoon fishing" as part of its prerogatives". (Urvoas, 2013a)

But the dismissal of Le Monde's account did not only come from policy-makers. Jean Marc Manach, a journalist, surveillance expert and privacy advocate, also bemoaned the paranoid tone of Le Monde's journalists (Manach, 2013). He also stressed that many of Le Monde's claims, which quoted some of his own reports on the DGSE's so-called "Frenchelon" program, were in fact not new and had been documented before. Manach was right. By then, officials from the DGSE had already hinted at the formidable growth of the agency's Internet surveillance capabilities. In 2010, its Chief Technology Officer, Bernard Barbier, who was then supervising the plan agreed upon in Sarkozy's office two years earlier, boasted during a public talk before the Cryptographers' Reserve that France was in the "first division" of communications intelligence. He also revealed that the Internet was now the DGSE's "main target" (Manach, 2010). Then, in March 2013, just a few weeks before the beginning of the Snowden disclosures, the head of the DGSE was even less equivocal, admitting before the National Assembly that, since 2008, "we have been able to develop a significant plan for the surveillance of Internet traffic" (French National Assembly, 2013).

### Advocacy Failure

This, in turn begs the question of why, in the immediate aftermath of the Snowden disclosures and even prior to that, it took so long for human rights groups in France to pick up on the pieces of information already available and go after these illegal surveillance operations, both in courts and in policy-making arenas. The question is a complex one, and cannot be fully addressed here. But two aspects deserve to be mentioned. First, regarding strategic litigation, it is worth noting that in the French civil law system, legal opportunities have traditionally been lacking (Meili, 1998), especially in a field such as state surveillance covered by state secrets. Statements by officials are not enough to initiate legal action. In other countries like the US, they might help trigger successful "FOIA requests" (named after the 1966 Freedom of Information Act) (Schulhofer, 2015). In France however, the national "freedom of information" law adopted in 1978 has extremely broad national security exemptions and is generally much weaker (for instance, the request must specify the exact name of the documents sought after, which represents a formidable hurdle in policy areas covered by state secrets) (Chevallier, 1992).

Second, and more importantly, the lack of mobilisation prior and in the immediate aftermath of the first Snowden disclosures speaks about the structural weaknesses of online privacy advocacy in France, at least until late 2013. Even when in October 2013, thanks to the Snowden trove, Le Monde revealed the existence of the so-called LUSTRE data-sharing agreement between the NSA and the DGSE, showing that the latter sent millions of metadata records daily to the US agency (Follorou, 2013), human rights advocacy groups did not pick up on the issue. A few hypotheses, based on observant-participation conducted in this advocacy field, can be offered to explain these structural weaknesses. Though there have been recent and successful episodes of contention against offline surveillance and intelligence files, Internet surveillance has mostly remained out of the focus of large human rights organisations and smaller digital rights groups in the past decade, which may be due to the particular interests of their staff and subsequent prioritisation in handling their limited resources.

Also, a general knowledge of the field in the US, the UK or Germany suggests that historical factors, more recent legalisation processes and leaks regarding Internet surveillance programs likely played an important role in helping civil society groups in these countries maintain stronger networks and expertise. One major moment of the transnational post-Snowden contention, for instance, was the release of the "International Principles on the Application of Human Rights to Communications Surveillance" in May 2014 (EFF, 2014). Although framed as a key response of the global civil society to the Snowden controversies, the work on this text started as early as 2012 and, as noted in the document, "more than 40 privacy and security experts participated in the drafting process". However, according to one interview conducted for this article with a lawyer who played a major role in the drafting of this document, there wasn't any French national among them. This tends to confirm that, until recently, French NGOs had remained outside of these transnational networks working on state surveillance.

### Legalisation of Metadata Access Sparks Contention

These structural weaknesses of anti-surveillance advocacy in France help explain why intelligence policymakers would try to legalise very intrusive metadata access powers as early as October 2013, in the midst of the Snowden scandal. In 2006, a law had been adopted to give intelligence agencies access to metadata records held by access providers and hosting providers, but only for fighting terrorism. What is more, from 2009 on, intelligence agencies had apparently experimented with traffic-scanning devices provided by Qosmos and installed on the infrastructure of the few major telecom operators to monitor metadata in real-time (Hourdeaux, 2016; Reflets. info, 2016). Already in late-2012, it was becoming clear to intelligence policy experts that—in line with what had already been alluded to in the 2008 White Paper of Defence—these crucial capabilities for expanded and real-time access to metadata needed to be secured. Despite public discussions on the matter in Parliament at the time, nobody in the advocacy sphere apparently took notice.

In August 2013, Prime Minister Manuel Valls presented the 2014–2019 Military Planning Bill (Loi de Programmation Militaire, or LPM). Over the course of the parliamentary debate, and in particular when the Senate adopted amendments to the Bill in first reading in October 2013, the law became the vehicle for a partial legalisation of the new capabilities. We were just four months after the first Snowden disclosures, and again no human rights organisation reacted. Six weeks later however, an industry group representing online social services including Google France, AOL, eBay, Facebook, Microsoft, Skype and French companies like Deezer or Dailymotion published an article against the reform (Association des Services Internet Communautaires, 2013). It was only then that human rights groups understood the importance of this provision and mounted a last-minute effort to get the provision out of the bill.

Coming at a very late stage of the legislative procedure, the effort eventually failed to strike out the provision. But despite this failure and a somewhat exaggerated denunciation of "generalised surveillance," this first episode of post-Snowden contention had at last led to the mobilisation of civil society groups around Internet surveillance issues, one which benefited from widespread media coverage. Frustrated by their failure to react in time (before rather than after industry groups) and also finally realising the need to build and share expertise around Internet surveillance and digital rights in general, human rights groups created a new umbrella organisation. Announced on the international "data protection day" in January 2014, it was called the Observatoire des Libertés et du Numérique (OLN). OLN's initial members included organisations that often worked together on non-Internet issues—including the Human Rights League, a lawyers' union (Syndicat des Avocats de France) and a judges' union (Syndicat de la Magistrature). They were joined by two smaller research organisations devoted to the interplay of the digital technologies and privacy (CECIL and CREIS-Terminal).

A few days later, LQDN—with its already established expertise on digital rights, its singular Internet-inspired political culture as well as its own international networks (Breindl, 2011)—, asked to join the coalition. This brokerage of new connections between French human rights NGOs would play a key role against the Intelligence Bill. But in the meantime, the government apparently slowed the path to legalisation set forth by Urvoas in its recent reports. Post-Snowden contention was finally under way in France, and it was likely perceived to make any significant intelligence reform much more politically risky. At least in the short term.

## A Long-Awaited Legalisation: Passing the 2015 Intelligence Act

Soon, with the spectacular rise of the threat posed by the Islamic State (Giroux, 2014) and the Paris attacks of January 2015, "securitisation" discourses helped create the adequate political conditions for the passage of the Intelligence Act—the most extensive piece of legislation ever adopted in France to regulate the work of intelligence agencies. Securitisation is understood in critical security studies as "speech acts through which an intersubjective understanding is constructed within a political community to treat something as an existential threat to a valued referent object, and to enable a call for urgent and exceptional measures to deal with the threat" (Buzan &Wæver, 2003, p. 491). In the field of terrorism, these areof course not new. And by the time the Intelligence Bill was introduced, anti-terrorism was already back on the top of the political agenda in France, with the looming threat coming from the Islamic State in Syria and Iraq.

In July 2014, just as the government was introducing a new anti-terrorism bill before the Parliament, President François Hollande convened a National Intelligence Council at the Élysée Palace. In the laconic press-release issued on that day, the Council claimed to have "determined the strategic priorities of [intelligence] services and approved the legal, technical and human resources necessary to carry on these priorities" (French Presidency, 2014). The debate on the anti-terrorism bill, finally adopted on November 2014, also gave an opportunity to OLN members to engage in their first coordinated action against the law's new restrictions on freedom of expression online. But on January 25th 2015, then Prime Minister Manuel Valls turned the long-awaited intelligence reform into an essential part of the government's political response to the Paris attacks carried on earlier that month. With the country under shock, Valls presented yet another package of "exceptional measures" that formed part of the government's proclaimed "general mobilisation against terrorism". (French Government, 2015).

He announced his government would soon present a new bill, which he said was "necessary to strengthen the legal capacity of intelligence agencies to act," alluding to "Djihadist Internet communications". The Paris attacks only reinforced the ongoing trend toward securitisation, helping to locate the fight against terrorism—and the instrumental role of communications surveillance in that respect—beyond the domain of normal, democratic politics. Securitisation would for instance justify the government's choice to present the bill to Parliament using a fast-track procedure, allowing only one ruling in each of the Parliament's chambers. In sum securitisation was effectively added to denials as rhetorical strategies aimed at dealing with post-Snowden contention, and finally pass a legal basis for what were until then illegal security practices.

### The Intelligence Act's Main Provisions on Internet Surveillance

During the expeditious parliamentary debate that ensued (April–June 2015), the bill's proponents never missed an opportunity to stress, as Valls did while presenting the text to the National Assembly, that the new law had "nothing to do with the practices revealed by Edward Snowden". Distinction strategies notwithstanding, the Act's provisions actually demonstrate how important the sort of practices revealed by Snowden have become for the geopolitical "arms race" in communications intelligence. The Intelligence Act creates whole new sections in the Code of Internal Security. It starts off by widening the scope of public-interest motives for which surveillance can be authorised. Besides terrorism, economic intelligence, organised crime and counter-espionage, it now includes vague notions such as the promotion of "major interests in foreign policy" or the prevention of "collective violence likely to cause serious harm to public peace". As for the number of agencies allowed to use this new legal basis for extra-judicial surveillance, it comprises the "second circle" of law enforcement agencies that are not part of the official "intelligence community" and whose combined staff is well over 45,000. In terms of technical capabilities, the Act seeks to harmonise the range of tools that intelligence agencies can use on the regime applicable to judicial investigations.

These include targeted telephone and Internet wiretaps, access to metadata and geotagging records as well as computer intrusion and exploitation (i.e. "hacking"). But the Act also authorises techniques that directly echo the large-scale surveillance practices at the heart of post-Snowden controversies. Such is the case of the so-called "black boxes", these scanning devices that will use Big Data techniques to sort through Internet traffic in order to detect "weak signals" of terrorism (intelligence officials have given the example of encryption as the sort of things these black boxes would be looking for). Another provision limited to anti-terrorism allows for the real-time collection of metadata. Initially, the provision targeted only individuals "identified as a [terrorist] threat". After the 2016 Nice attack, it was extended to cover individuals "likely related to a threat" or who simply belong to "the entourage" of individuals "likely related to a threat". In theory, tens of thousands of people could fall under this definition, and have their metadata collected in real-time during a renewable period of four months.

Similarly, there is a whole chapter on "international surveillance", which legalises the massive programme deployed by the DGSE since 2008 to tap into international cables. Like in other countries, the underlying logic of this article breaches the universality of human rights: "communications crossing French borders can be intercepted and analysed "in bulk" with lesser safeguards than those applicable to domestic surveillance. However, the transnational nature of the Internet makes it very likely that the communications of French citizens and residents massively end up in the DGSE's nets, despite a pledge for procedures of so-called "technical minimisation" aimed at protecting communications related to "French technical identifiers" (e.g. French IP addresses). The Act also grants blanket immunity to intelligence officers who carry on computer crimes into computer systems located abroad, which again will directly affect many French Internet users. The provision may contravene Article 32(b) of the Budapest Convention on Cybercrime on the trans-border access to computer data (Cybercrime Convention Committee, 2014).

This provision speaks to the fact that, with encryption on the rise since 2013, the capability to massively penetrate endpoints through hacking is becoming a focus point for intelligence agencies (e.g. UK Home Office, 2016). As for oversight, as it has been the case since the 1991 Wiretapping Act, all national surveillance activities are authorised by the Prime Minister. A revamped oversight commission (the CNCTR) composed of judges and members of Parliament has 24 hours to issue nonbinding opinions on authorisation requests. The main innovation of the Intelligence Act is the creation of a new redress mechanism before the Conseil d'Etat (France's Supreme Court for administrative law), but the procedure is veiled in secrecy and fails to respect defence rights, which again echoes the law of the US and the UK (Bigo, Carrera, Hernanz, & Scherrer, 2014). International surveillance will remain completely outside of this redress procedure. Among other notable provisions, one forbids the oversight body from reviewing communications data obtained from foreign agencies. The law also fails to provide any framework to regulate (and limit) access to the collected intelligence once it is stored by intelligence and law enforcement agencies, thereby running counter to recent rulings by the Court of Justice of the European Union (CJEU) (Woods, 2016).

### Mobilisation against the Controversial French

Intelligence Bill By the time the Intelligence Bill was debated in Parliament in April 2015, human rights organisations partnering in OLN had built the kind of networking and expertise that made them more suited to campaign against national security legislation. They led the contention during the three-month-long parliamentary debate on the Bill, acting as the core of a network of actors typical of post-Snowden contention, including international partners in the NGO world, groups of scientists, engineers and hacker groups, French independent companies from the digital sector, and even a few security experts (including former intelligence analysts or a former anti-terrorist judge). These actors also received backing from leading national and international human rights organisations (data protection agency, Council of Europe, UN special rapporteurs, etc.). Interestingly, to the contrary of the full-fledged contention waged in the US or the UK, large US technology firms like Google or Microsoft declined to engage in the French debate, perhaps out of fear for being cornered for their double-speak on privacy and antagonising French officials, who regularly accused them of engaging in intrusive forms of commercial surveillance. As for their French competitors, like telecommunications companies Orange, SFR and others, their even greater dependence on and proximity with the state political elite probably explain why they chose to remain neutral bystanders.

Overall, contention played an important role in barring amendments that would have given intelligence agencies even more leeway than originally afforded by the bill. Whereas the government hoped for a union sacrée, contention also managed to fracture the initial display of unanimity. MPs from across the political spectrum (including several within both socialist and conservative ranks) fought against the bill, pushing its proponents to amend the text in order to bring significant safeguards compared to the government's proposal. However, the general philosophy of the text remained intact. In June 2015, the bill was eventually adopted with 438 votes in favour, 86 against and 42 abstentions at the National Assembly and 252 for, 67 against and 26 abstentions at the Senate. The implementation decrees were adopted by the government between October 2015 and

February 2016, giving civil society opponents a two-month window to introduce several important legal challenges before the Council of State which are, at the time of writing, still pending. Other legal challenges have been introduced before the ECHR.

## Conclusion: Facing the Snowden Paradox

The first Snowden disclosures and the global scandal that followed held the promise of an upcoming rollback of the techno-legal apparatus developed by the NSA, the GCHQ and their counterparts to intercept and analyse large portions of the world's Internet traffic. State secrets and the "plausible deniability" doctrine often used by these secretive organisations could no longer stand in the face of such overwhelming documentation. Intelligence reform, one could then hope, would soon be put on the agenda to relocate these surveillance programmes within the boundaries of the rule of law. Almost four years later, however, what were then reasonable expectations have likely been crushed. Intel- ligence reform is being passed, but mainly to secure the legal basis for large-scale surveillance to a degree of detail that was hard to imagine just a few years ago. Despite unprecedented mobilisations against surveillance practices developed in the shadows of the "deep state", the latter are progressively being legalised. Hence the Snowden paradox.

France was the first liberal regime to engage in a sweeping, post-Snowden intelligence reform. There, even prior to 2013, the legal pressure exerted by human rights standards, and their application by supranational courts like the ECHR, had already triggered a slow process of legalisation. Post-Snowden contention only made that pressure stronger, pushing intelligence policymakers to secure and expand the surveillance capabilities of their agencies through intelligence reform, as soon as the political conditions seemed ripe. While it would be tempting to see the Intelligence Act of 2015 as part of a certain French tradition when it comes to regulating the Internet (Mailland, 2001; Meyer & Audenhove, 2012; Tréguer, 2015), the situation in other countries suggests that the French case is part of a wider trend. In the Fall of 2016, the British Parliament passed the much-criticised Investigatory Powers Bill (Hintz & Dencik, 2016). Simultaneously in Germany, amendments to the so-called "G-10 law" were adopted to validate the large-scale surveillance powers of the country's foreign intelligence agency, the BND— also embroiled in the NSA scandal (Wetzling, 2016).

In the Netherlands, an ongoing intelligence reform is raising similar concerns, while the reform of the US PATRIOT Act in June 2015 was extremely modest. Detailed crosscountry comparisons are of course warranted. But despite important variations between these countries—for instance regarding the initial weaknesses and strengths of privacy advocacy in these different national contexts, or the role played by large US Internet firms in policy debates—, these other instances of post-Snowden intelligence reform seem to confirm the existence of the Snowden paradox. Fifteen years after 9/11, which brought an abrupt end to the controversy on the NSA's ECHELON program (Campbell, 2000) and paved the way for the adoption of the PATRIOT Act in the US and similar legislation elsewhere, the threat of terrorism and associated processes of securitisation are hindering the global episode of contention opened by Edward Snowden. Securitisation creates a "chilling effect" on civil society contention, making legalisation politically possible and leading to a "ratchet effect" in the development of previously illegal security practices or, more generally, of executive powers.

In that regard, post-Snowden intelligence reform stands as a stark reminder of the fact that, once coupled with securitisation, "a-legality" and national security become two convenient excuses for legalisation and impunity, allowing states to navigate the legal and political constraints created by human rights organisations and institutional pluralism. During the debate on the French Intelligence Act, Urvoas stressed that the law was neither Schmitt's nor Agamben's states of exception (Urvoas, 2013b). But because it is "legal" or includes some oversight and redress mechanisms does not mean that large-scale surveillance and secret procedures do not represent a formidable challenge to the rule of law. Rather than a state of exception, legalisation carried on under the guise of the raison d'État amounts to what Sidney Tarrow calls "rule by law". In his comparative study of the relationships between states, wars and contention, he writes of the US "war on terror":

Is the distinction between rule of law and rule by law a distinction without difference? I think not. First, rule by law convinces both decision makers and operatives that their illegal behavior is legally protected....Second, engaging in rule by law provides a defense against the charge they are breaking the law. Over time, and repeated often enough, this can create a "new normal", or at least a new content for long-legitimated symbols of the American creed. Finally, "legalizing" illegality draws resources and energies away from other forms of contention. (2015, pp. 165–166) The same process is happening with regards to present day state surveillance: the suspicionless interception of communications, "big data" preventive policing and large-scale computer hacking are becoming the new normal in intelligence practices. At this point in time, it seems difficult to argue that post-Snowden contention has hindered in any significant and lasting way the formidable growth of surveillance capabilities of the world's most powerful intelligence agencies.

And yet, while the current trend of legalisation is especially worrying considering the ongoing illiberal drift in Western democracies, the jury is still out. Besides legalisation, Post-Snowden contention is having another major outcome: new coordination in civil society both nationally and globally, with the formation of a transnational movement against Internet surveillance (Tarrow, 2016). This emerging movement has been documenting Internet surveillance like never before, undermining some of the secrecy that surrounds the intelligence field and hinders its democratic accountability. It has provided fresh political and legal arguments to reclaim privacy as a "part of the common good" (Lyon, 2015, p. 9), and helped push for the proliferation of legal and policy recommendations regarding the compliance of surveillance with human rights. Most crucially, this emerging privacy movement has led courts—in particular the ECHR and the CJEU—to consider cases of historic importance that, in the long run, could prove to be game-changers. Strategic litigation has indeed the potential of turning the Snowden paradox on its head, that is to use these new laws—and the new legal opportunities it brings to privacy advocates— to counter the surveillance practices that legalisation sought to legitimise in the first place. Judges now appear as the last institutional resort against large-scale surveillance. If court actions fail, the only possibility left for resistance will lie in what would by then represent a most transgressive form of political action: democratising the use of strong encryption, and subverting the centralised and commodified technical architecture that made such surveillance possible in the first place.

*Acknowledgements: This research was conducted for the UTIC project, supported by the French National Research Agency. Conflict of Interests: The author declares no conflict of interests. Article: Intelligence Reform and the Snowden Paradox: The Case of France. Félix Tréguer, Center for International Studies and Research, Sciences Po, 75006 Paris, France; E-Mail: felix.treguer@sciencespo.fr, Félix Tréguer works on past and present contention around the protection of civil rights and communicational autonomy on the Internet. He is a junior researcher at CERI-Sciences Po, where he looks at post-Snowden controversies for the UTIC project. He is a founding member of the Paris-based digital rights advocacy group La Quadrature du Net. Submitted: 10 November 2016 | Accepted: 26 January 2017 | Published: 22 March 2017 Focus* and Scope: Media and Communication is an international open access journal dedicated to a wide variety of basic and applied research in communication and its related fields. It aims at providing a research forum on the social and cultural relevance of media and communication processes. Media and Communication is concerned with the social development and contemporary transformation of media and communication and critically reflects on their interdependence with global, individual, media, digital, economic and visual processes of change and innovation. Contributions ponder the social, ethical, and cultural conditions, meanings and consequences of media, the public sphere and organizational as well as interpersonal communication and their complex interrelationships. The journal focuses on the application and advancement of qualitative and quantitative methods of media and communication research, but also encourages scholars to submit manuscripts that introduce innovative and alternative theoretical perspectives. Media and Communication presents up-to-date international research results stressing, but not being restricted to, topics of media and professionalism in public communication, mass media and politics, participatory communication processes, systems and cultures. It is open to proposals for special issues, commentaries, book reviews and extended review essays. Media and Communication (ISSN: 2183-2439). 2017, Volume 5, Issue 1, Pages 17–28. DOI: 10.17645/mac.v5i1.821. Issue: This article is part of the issue "Post-Snowden Internet Policy", edited by Julia Pohle (WZB Berlin Social Science Center, Germany) and Leo Van Audenhove (Vrije Universiteit Brussel, Belgium). © 2017 by the author; licensee Cogitatio (Lisbon, Portugal). This article is licensed under a Creative Commons Attribution 4.0 International License (CC BY).

Peer Review Process: Manuscripts will undergo a very stringent double-blind peer-review process, where the identities of authors, reviewers and editors remain undisclosed in order to guarantee the highest quality of the journal. All manuscripts (except for Editorials, Commentaries, and Book Reviews) will be sent out for review and at least two review reports per manuscript will be collected. All reviewers will be carefully selected by the journal's Editors for each submitted manuscript and must fulfill the following criteria: Hold a PhD degree and/or be a recognized expert in the field; Not have co-authored publications with the author(s) for the last 5 years; Not be affiliated with the same institution as the author(s). Even if, in principle, a double-blind peer-review system could allow this task to be performed by scholars who are acquainted with the authors, our Editorial Office still wishes reviews to be completed only by reviewers who do not have any recent professional contact with the authors in order to fully guarantee that there are no conflicts of interests and that reviews are indeed totally unbiased. Spontaneous applications from scholars to join the journal's pool of reviewers will not be considered. All reviewers will be selected and invited by the Editorial Office to review manuscripts according to the field of expertise of the submissions received. Reviewers will be asked to complete their review within two weeks, but are allowed to extend the review period in order to complete and submit their report. All relevant information for reviewers can be consulted in the Instructions for Reviewers. Open Access Policy. This journal provides immediate open access to its content on the principle that making research *freely available to the public supports a greater global exchange of knowledge. All of our journals are open access, that is, they can be accessed free of charge by any reader, anywhere in the world, regardless of affiliation. This means that not only researchers backed by well-funded institutions, but also policy-makers, NGOs, journalists, practitioners, students, and an interested public have free access to the research articles. This increases the exposure gained by new works and allows them to be disseminated to a much wider audience than is possible through traditional subscription journals. Open access publication also helps correct the information bias towards the developed world, where institutions are much more likely to have the resources to subscribe to journals than elsewhere. Cogitatio Press is committed to the democratisation of knowledge, and open access means that any researcher from any institution, anywhere in the world is able to access the full extent of our publications with no subscription fees. Furthermore, unlike traditional journals, Cogitatio Press does not assume copyright for articles published through open access. This means that the authors retain the copyright to their own works and are free to distribute them as they wish. Once again, this allows authors to maximise the audience their works are able to reach, rather than tying them to a limited audience of subscribers. Journal Contact: Mailing Address. Cogitatio Press Rua Fialho de Almeida 14, 2º Esq. 1070-129 Lisbon. Portugal. Principal Contact. Raquel Silva Cogitatio Press Rua Fialho de Almeida 14, 2º Esq. 1070-129 Lisbon Portugal. Email: mac@cogitatiopress. com. Support Contact Media and Communication ; Email: mac@cogitatiopress.com. Media and Communication. Open Access Journal. ISSN: 2183-2439*

## Chapter 7

# Espionage by Europeans: Treason and Counterintelligence in Post-Cold War Europe

*Michael Jonsson*

**Abstract**

As war rages in Ukraine, counterintelligence has again taken center-stage for European intelligence agencies. In spite of the long-ascendant espionage threat, to date little is known about who is recruited, what motivated them and how they were caught. This article presents an analysis of espionage against European NATO and/or EU members, based on court convictions in 2010–2021. This provides a first overview of contemporary espionage in Europe, and complements previous research, which is dominated by single-case studies, mainly of Anglo-Saxon cases. Replicating large-N studies of American espionage, the study identifies transatlantic commonalities, including perpetrators being overwhelmingly male, middle-aged, and a mainly working outside of defence or intelligence agencies. But also differences, with Russia being by far the main instigator of espionage in Europe, a strong concentration of cases in Northern Europe, and a diversity of legislation coinciding with equally variable outcomes in court. Generally, the similarities speak to the nature of contemporary espionage, whereas the differences are chiefly attributable to geopolitical differences between the US and Europe.

Keywords Espionage Europe EU NATO counterintelligence recruitment Russia GRU FSB SVR China Iran.

## Introduction

With the Russian invasion of Ukraine on 24 February 2022, the comparatively peaceful post-Cold War era has ended. But years before Russian troops crossed Ukrainian borders, scholars discussed the fall of the 'liberal world order', and the gradual end to American unipolar hegemony on the international stage.[1] Consequently, China and Russia have eclipsed transnational terrorism as a security threat to the USA and intelligence scholars are arguing that offensive Humint–recruiting foreign spies – should again play a primary role.[2] While not disputing this – quite to the contrary – this article explores a key corollary, namely that counterintelligence (CI) is swiftly becoming equally crucial. That is, if we need human sources to access the 'most important secrets (…) likely contained either in the minds of a select few or in heavily guarded vaults' of authoritarian adversaries, safeguarding our own should be equally vital, particularly given the openness of Western societies.[3] After all, the former chief of CIA Counterintelligence James Olson noted in 2021 that '[a]t no time in my career have I considered the challenges for US counterintelligence greater than they are right now'.[4] Similarly, intelligence officials and scholars alike have been raising alarms over espionage against Europe – particularly by Russia,[5] but increasingly also China.[6]

The global shift from the post-Cold War liberal international order and back to geopolitical confrontation is particularly palpable in contemporary Europe. After the Warsaw Pact dissolved, central and eastern European countries gradually liberalized and joined the EU, making erstwhile adversaries stakeholders in the regional peace project. For two decades after the fall of the Berlin Wall, European politicians exhorted a sense of optimism–about the European project itself, but also the positive impact it was having on aspiring members. Reflecting its largely liberal foreign policy outlook, military security and counterintelligence took a back seat to non-state threats, and counterterrorism became the main priority of Western intelligence agencies. In spite of the Russo-Georgian war in 2008, this outlook has been slow to change in large parts of Europe, even as Russia's European neighbors warned of its revisionist intentions.[7] However, as geopolitical tensions have risen, the active measures, election meddling, disinformation campaigns and recruitment of spies by antagonistic intelligence agencies against both the US and Europe have become increasingly blatant.[8]

In hindsight, it is easy to agree that years of attempted murders of European citizens, explosions at munitions depots, and extrajudicial executions of defectors did indeed amount to an 'undeclared war' waged by the Russian intelligence agencies, as Keir Giles pointed out.[9] Commenting on a string of espionage cases instigated by Russia in Europe, Mark Galeotti also noted that 'The Russian intelligence community is now operating with a war-time mind-set'.[10] In a similar vein, northern European intelligence agencies have long been sounding the alarm, noting a growing espionage threat, particularly from Russia and China.[11] In spite of this, the espionage threat against Europe remains surprisingly poorly understood, especially compared to our relatively detailed understanding of the situation in the US. Importantly, in the absence of continent-wide comparative studies, it is not possible to spot regional patterns, trends over time, the modus of antagonistic intelligence agencies, and so forth. While there is a series of reports analyzing how the espionage threat against the US has evolved over the past seven decades – based on analysis of over 200 convictions on espionage charges – no comparable study of Europe exists. This article represents a first step towards addressing this research lacuna.[12]

## Empirical Evidence of Espionage in Europe

Comparative studies of espionage are few and far between. Traditionally, research on the perpetrators of espionage has instead centered on in-depth single-case studies, primarily of Anglo-Saxon spies.[13] Given the complexity of the subject, and the dearth of reliable, readily accessible sources, this is understandable. But is also regrettable, as the absence of large-N studies– complementing the insightful case studies of paradigmatic cases such as Ames, Hansen, Philby, Walker, McLean and so forth – may skew our understanding of who spies, what motivated them, and how they were recruited.[14] In 1997, Taylor & Snow published a landmark study outlining the motives of 139 Americans who were officially charged with spying against their government, during or immediately following the end of the Cold War.[15] One of their findings was that Aldrich Ames – the infamous CIA mole caught in 1994 – might have been more difficult to identify because CI officials had pre-conceived notions of spies' motives.[16]

In the Ames case, investigators may have been influenced by the profile of Cold War spies, who were more often motivated by ideology, while Ames – like many of his contemporaries – was mainly driven by greed.[17] This demonstrates a simple but fundamental methodological point. In-depth case studies are highly useful for a variety of purposes, such as illustrating the complexity of investigating suspected moles, the multitude of overlapping motives that may drive them, recounting how recruitment can evolve over long periods of time, or the oddly affectionate relationship that some spies develop to their handlers. None of this can easily be illustrated in quantitative studies, or conveyed by statistics alone. Reversely, single-case studies offers us no way of discerning how representative a specific case is for the broader population of spies, or even the extent and composition of that population. Hence, both avenues of research are clearly needed, and mutually complementary.[18]

The Taylor and Snow study was followed by four studies by Katherine L Herbig and colleagues at the Defense Personnel and Security Research Center of the U.S. Department of Defence.[19] In the latest edition of the report, the study includes 209 cases, spanning the period 1947–2015, of which 67 occurred during the 1990–2015 period. Among numerous insights, the study demonstrates for example that China has overtaken Russia as the main instigator of espionage against the US, that the vast majority of convicted spies are male and that monetary gains remains the most common motive, but less so than in earlier cohorts. Furthermore, only one-quarter of the convicted spies were military, and compared to earlier cohorts, increasing proportions were contractors, held jobs unrelated to espionage, and/or did not hold security clearances.[20] By designing a structured dataset, disaggregated by different time-periods, and compiling data on everything from personal motives to the socio-economic backgrounds of recruits, this series established a gold standard for comparatives research on espionage.

To date there is no comparable study of espionage in contemporary Europe.[21] Instead, there is a handful of comparative articles analyzing large-N samples of espionage within individual jurisdictions, at different periods in time. For instance, Jurvee and Perling published a survey of Russian espionage cases in Estonia. The sample includes 20 individuals convicted in 2009–2019, of which all but one was male. Three convicts had a background from the Estonian Internal Security Service (ISS) and one was an army officer, and these four individuals received notably harsher sentencing than the rest of the sample, presumably reflecting the gravity of their betrayal.[22] Lillbacka studied 285 cases compiled from Finland (1945–1977), Sweden (1939–1942) and the U.S. (1975–2008), to test statistically the proposition that ideologically motivated spies 'originate primarily from socio-culturally coherent groups where beliefs that are directly or indirectly favorable to a foreign power are prevalent'.

Simplifying matters, the study found strong support for the hypothesis, while also finding i.a. results that were 'clearly consistent with the notion that non-ideological spies will manifest more "pathological" markers', for instance revenge motives, previous crimes and personal problems. Hence, as best we can tell, there are some systematic differences between ideological and non-ideological spies.[23] Less germane to this article, Macrakis has analysed the impact of espionage by Stasi spies on the scientific and technological development of East Germany during the Cold War[24] and some international databases compile a partial selection of contemporary espionage cases, including from Europe.[25] However, there is nothing approaching a comparative study of contemporary espionage against European countries, similar to what Herbig and colleagues have done for the US.

This article attempts to remedy this, by compiling data on cases of espionage in Europe during the past decade (2010–2021). To enable comparisons with American cases, the variable selection and coding practises largely replicate Herbig et al, although it should be emphasized early on that the data – compiled mainly through secondary sources – are often much thinner than in the original study. Minor adjustments were also made to adapt the research design to a European context, adding a few new variables of interest. Specifically, where possible, not only the country, but also the specific intelligence agency instigating espionage is noted. To make the study manageable in scope, data collection is focused on European NATO and/or EU members, all in all 33 countries.[26] As opposed to research on espionage in individual jurisdictions, cases were selected both on whether a specific act is defined as espionage in the jurisdiction where an individual was convicted, and whether this conforms with a rudimentary definition of espionage, i.e., procuring classified or sensitive information, making contact with a foreign recipient and handing over the information.[27]

Even minor adjustments to the criteria could have expanded the sample. For instance, in Sweden alone, several individuals have been convicted for sharing sensitive military information in closed online fora. But absent a foreign instigator, they were convicted of unauthorized access to classified data (Sw. obehörig befattning med hemlig uppgift), not espionage, and hence excluded here.[28] There were plenty of cases that prompted discussions on proper delimitations – too numerous to recount in full – and other researchers might have made different distinctions, expanding or shrinking the sample marginally. The study, however explicitly excludes cyber and diaspora espionage, as well as so-called illegals, signals intelligence (SIGINT) and disinformation campaigns, whereas economic espionage using human sources is included.[29] Again, these choices are purposely similar to Herbig et al, to ensure comparability between the samples.

As the first attempt to study a complex and potentially enormous subject, the gaps and possible sources of error of the data must be acknowledged upfront, beyond delimitations and case selection. Firstly, the study relies exclusively on open, secondary sources. While open sources was an inherent requirement, the possibility of conducting complementary interviews was precluded due to the global COVID-19 pandemic. Secondly, European countries vary dramatically in how much data is reported in the public domain on espionage cases. For instance, Baltic cases were broadly reported in long-form journalistic accounts (often including interviews with perpetrators), whereas the author frequently struggled to ascertain the outcomes in Polish cases, and far fewer details were reported. This implies that the granularity of data – narrative and quantitative – varies greatly between cases.[30]

Thirdly, when espionage is detected, national authorities can to choose whether to press charges – and hence make the case public – or use more discreet methods, such as removing access to classified information for the suspected spy, or declaring foreign intelligence officers persona non grata.[31] Hence, the study should not be read as measuring the espionage threat against individual European countries, nor as an evaluation of national counterintelligence efforts, as the espionage cases that eventually reach court in most likely represent merely the tip of the iceberg. That said, the study covers the vast majority of convictions on (state-centric) espionage in Europe during the 2010s, and systematically organizes and analyses them in considerable detail. This is key, as it enables us to spot regional patterns, trends over time and antagonists' modus, revealing several novel findings. Crucially, several of the trends are so strong that the addition of a limited number of cases would only alter the main results marginally, if at all.[32]

Based on these criteria, 42 individuals convicted on espionage in Europe in 2010–2021 were identified, with the full sample presented. Of these, 30 began spying after 2010 (category A), whereas another 12 began their espionage prior to 2010, but were convicted in 2010–2021 (category B). In this article, the analysis is focused on these 42 individuals, with a full list of cases. Beyond this, another 13 suspected spies, that had not yet been tried in court by the end of 2021 were identified (category C), and another 7 included in a miscellaneous category (D).[33] Although the aim was to identify and include every case that fulfils the criteria, these 42 individuals represent the majority of convicted European spies, but cases may still have been omitted. To be clear, the data set is a compilation of failed espionage, insofar that perpetrators were caught eventually. As such, less-skilled spies might be inadvertently over-represented. However, crucially, regional patterns of convictions may also say as much about counterintelligence efforts (and policy, i.e., whether to prosecute or not) as they do about the underlying espionage threat.

## Transatlantic similarities

When analysed as a whole, there are some notable similarities between American and European spies. Firstly, almost the entire European contingent–40 out of 42 spies – was male. In fact, the only two females were both married to other convicted spies. Firstly, the wife of Aleksei Dressen – a mid-level Estonian Internal Security Service officer (Est: Kaitsepolitseiamet, KAPO). Dressen was reportedly recruited sometime in 1998–2001, while visiting his wife's relatives in Russia, and stolen information was at time delivered by her while travelling to Russia on business.[34] And secondly, the wife of a German-Afghan translator was convicted alongside her husband, with her 'aiding and abetting' the espionage on behalf of Iran.[35] Both were hence accomplices to their husbands' crimes, rather than the principal perpetrators, and received more lenient sentencing.[36] In fact, even in our broader sample, all women suspected seemingly worked in husband-wife teams. This includes the wives of two suspect spies under investigation at the time of writing (in Germany [37] and Bulgaria[38]), and two wives in Russian 'illegals' couples (albeit in these cases, the veracity of the marriages themselves can be questioned).[39] Husband-wife teams were not unheard of in the American population of spies either,[40] but there were also women acting as the principal spies and working alone, or together with other female spies.[41]

Espionage being a predominantly male crime dovetails well with findings from the US. Herbig for instance finds that 91 per cent of convicted American spies in 1990–2015 were male (92.5 per cent for the entire 1947–2015 period).[42] Why this is the case is however less well explored. Herbig argues that in the US men are over-represented amongst those holding security clearances; are more prone towards high-risk behavior; and over-represented in certain categories of criminality.[43] While continent-wide statistics for these indicators are hard to come by, these explanations are tentatively plausible in a European context as well. However, the possibility that female spies are less likely to be detected and convicted–due to either greater skills or receiving less CI scrutiny–of course cannot be excluded.

Like in the US, European spies typically also began at a relatively mature age. In America, between 1990–2015, the median age was just north of

40,[44] whereas in the Old World, the median was just below that.[45] Granted, there is a wide variance (between 18 and 64), but as a group, spies begin late compared to first-time offenders in many other crime categories. There can be a bias, insofar that spies may be detected well into their clandestine 'careers', or that prosecutions may focus on the latter parts of espionage, which may be easier to prove. That said, 'late onset espionage' mirrors recent patterns from the US, whereas in the 1980s, the median age was lower, skewed by an influx of young military spies.[46] To some extent, the middle-aged spy may reflect opportunities, as mid-career professionals are generally granted better access to classified or sensitive information over time, making them of greater interests to recruiters. Others may have experienced career disappointments, making them susceptible to recruitment, as may postings or business trips abroad, particularly to hostile countries. For instance, Dressen was demoted at least once prior to recruitment and disappointed in his career. Another ISS colleague, decorated Officer Vladimir Kulikov, was forced to leave the agency against his will due to language requirements, and later turned. Both men were recruited while visiting Russia.[47]

Age-wise, there is of course variance in the sample, with a group of low-level Estonian-Russian criminals recruited forcibly at a young age, [48] and others recruited young and then progressing in their careers, becoming more valuable assets. One example of the latter was the Estonian army officer Deniss Metsavas. Born in 1980, Metsavas was recruited through a honey trap of sorts while visiting relatives in Russia in 2007, and then blackmailed into remaining a GRU asset until his arrest in 2018 in Estonia. During the interim, Metsavas rose through the ranks of the Estonian army, gaining greater access to classified information, while also acting as a public spokesperson of sorts for Russian-speakers within the service.[49]

In terms of why Europeans betrayed their countries, the secondary data at our disposal varies greatly in granularity. In general, to study motives, in-depth interviews with perpetrators, in combination with other so-called motive indicators are typically necessary to arrive at well-founded conclusions.[50] Absent this opportunity, this article instead relies on secondary reporting, which in some cases was extensive and nuanced, and in others more limited. Either way, both self-reported motives and those ascribed by a prosecutor or judge, should be taken with a pinch of salt. Aggregating this data for the cases in which it was available, with results presented below, coercion was the most oft-cited reason, followed by monetary incentives. Coercion was at time elaborate, as when young

Estonian army officer Deniss Metsavas was lured into a honey trap, followed by fabricated rape allegations.

Years later, his father was also recruited as a courier, to persuade Metsavas to continue his espionage.[51] In most cases, however, it was very unceremonious, offering dual citizens who made a living as smugglers a choice between prison-time in Russia, or espionage against Estonia.[52] Coercion was however primarily used by Russian services, against individuals with either Russian citizenship or heritage.[53] This suggests that the stronger emphasis on coercion says more about the Russian modus – particularly when recruiting compatriots–than it does about the European context per se. Specifically, the Russian services recruited individuals dependent on being able to cross the border frequently–mainly because they resided in the border region, but some also had businesses or relatives in Russia.[54] This espionage was predominantly instigated by the FSB, who is responsible for border protection, and a majority of the assets were low-value spies.

Similarly, monetary rewards mattered to some recruits, but even the best-paid spies often had more complex and nuanced motives. For instance, an Austrian army colonel, active for over two decades, repeatedly travelled abroad to spend several days with his recruiter[55]; and a Portuguese counter-intelligence official was well paid–but also had a soft spot for Eastern European culture – and women.[56] Alongside Dressen, these were the only three cases where spies received more than €100 000 for their espionage, and none of them were a clear-cut example of greed alone. Hence, money clearly mattered, but seldom was the entire story. These tentative findings are interesting, as they partly overlap, and partly contrast, to motives for espionage in the US. In 1990–2015, American spies were primarily motivated either by money (37 per cent) or divided loyalties (35 percent), with coercion virtually non-existent.[57] As discussed above however, coercion was mainly a tool used by Russian services against individuals dependent on being able to visit Russia, exclusively in the Baltic States and not elsewhere.

Other psychosocial characteristics of the European spies are consistent with findings from the US, but less so with the classical espionage literature. For instance, there is little evidence that recruiters exploited some of the types of personal shortcomings often seen as vulnerabilities for recruitment.[58] Specifically, among European spies, there was no mention of psychosocial illness, drug abuse or gambling addiction and merely one instance of problematic drinking was reported.[59] This could of course be a result of having insufficiently granular data. Another possibility is also that security clearance procedures have been successful in sorting out would-be employees with some of these at least partly overtly observable problems. Furthermore, there was not a single mention of homosexuality being used to recruit spies.[60] There was however at least one instance where a heterosexual relation was exploited as a recruitment tool,[61] and hints that this might have occurred in other cases too.[62]

In terms of the MICE (Money, Ideology, Coercion, and Ego) model for recruitment, coercion and money hence seem to be most relevant in contemporary Europe. However, as discussed above, money is often part of the recruitment motive, but seldom its entirety.[63] In terms of ideology, it is difficult to discern cases of classically, ideologically motivated spies in the mould of Ana Montes (who spied for Cuba for 17 years) or Kim Philby (who spied for the Soviet Union for almost three decades), both without receiving any compensation. A possible hypothesis is that this is because the current Russian (or Chinese) political regimes scarcely can inspire same type of ideological commitment the Soviet Union did, or Cuba still may do. Lastly, like in the US, three quarters (31 of 42) of the European spies were civilians, i.e., neither uniformed military nor intelligence officials. In terms of the RASCL, i.e., on the tradecraft used to recruit spies, the data for most cases is much less granular. One aspect however stands out, insofar that more patient and elaborate tradecraft was used for a specific sub-set of recruits, primarily 'moles' inside defence or intelligence agencies. Arguably the most highly valued sources, recruiters overall paid greater amounts, used more elaborate tradecraft to protect them, and invested more time and energy in recruitment and retention of moles.[64] That said, and civilians were the most frequent recruits.

Cautiously, the similarities between US and European spies say something about the nature of contemporary espionage that is if not universal, then at least pervasive in Western societies. That is, the male and typically middle-aged spy seems to be a constant in espionage on both sides of the Atlantic, although the median age has varied more over time in the US.[65] Some of the possible explanations for why this is the case – opportunity, higher proclivity for high-risk criminality, the role as primary breadwinner, but also larger exposure to both recruitment attempts and CI scrutiny– have been outlined above, but cannot be fully disentangled here. That the majority of spies were recruited from the outside of the defence and intelligence establishments – which mirrors recent patterns in the US, but not earlier cohorts–is more intuitive, as vital security interests are today more dispersed than during the Cold War.[66] In the US, Herbig ascribes the trend of civilian spies partly to a growing number of contractors who have been hired and provided clearances. In Europe, part of the explanation is that a share of spies were used for minor tasks, such as mapping military infrastructure, troop movements or the like, assets of opportunity rather than pre-meditated recruitment targets.[67]

## Differences between European and American spies

In spite of these similarities, there are also numerous differences between European and American espionage. Most notably, in the 1990–2015 period, China overtook Russia as the main instigator of espionage against the US.[68] In Europe, Russia instead remained the by far greatest instigator, responsible for 37 out of 42 cases. In the 32 Russian cases where it was possible to pinpoint a specific security service, the GRU (14 individuals) and the FSB (15) were the most prolific, whereas SVR was responsible for only three recruitments.[69] Still more than Iran (2), Belarus (2) and China (1), however. This discrepancy between the espionage threat in Europe and the US clearly needs to be further explored. This is especially so given that the FBI and MI5 have jointly warned that China poses the primary intelligence threat against both the US and Europe.[70] A range of explanations is possible to hypothesize but difficult to test. One key factor is however presumably modus, with Chinese recruiters often occupying a grey zone, straddling the line between the inappropriate and the illegal.[71] For instance, there have been public allegations against heads of think tanks,[72] invitations to European parliamentarians to write 'political analysis' on the side,[73] the much-debated 'Thousand Talents' program,[74] and the even more polemic debate over Huawei.[75] Furthermore, whereas only one case instigated by China is included in the dataset, recently they are increasing.[76] To reiterate, this again highlights why convictions is an imperfect measure of the full range of the espionage threat, as much sensitive information may be extracted without necessarily crossing the threshold for what is prosecutable in court.

Hence, while Chinese espionage against Europe is ascendant – and receives increasing counterintelligence attention–Russia to date remains the main instigator behind cases that have led to court convictions in Europe. This includes a majority of the investigations underway. In fact, a single Russian service–the GRU–is reportedly suspected to have recruited at least 9 of the 13 suspected individuals in the 2010–2021 dataset. Beyond this, additional cases of suspected espionage in Europe on behalf of the GRU have come to light in 2022. This includes two Swedish-Iranian brothers–one of whom had worked both for the Swedish Security Service (Sw. SÄPO) and the Military Intelligence and Security Service (Sw. MUST)–convicted,[77] a Swedish-Russian couple arrested,[78] two Slovaks arrested,[79] and a German soldier[80] and a German officer of the foreign intelligence service (Ger. BND) arrested.[81] The large number of individuals convicted or suspected for espionage on behalf of Russia in 2022 is partly the result of Russia's war in Ukraine, with Russian services working in overdrive, and Western counterintelligence services responding in kind. But with so many of the recent cases reportedly involving espionage on behalf of the GRU, this inevitably raises questions as to whether the service itself may have been compromised.

The second difference vis-à-vis the US, is that espionage convictions in Europe are strongly clustered in the north-eastern part of the continent, with the nationality of convicted perpetrators summarized, above. Particularly the Baltic countries had a disproportionate share of the espionage cases. While these countries represent less than 2 per cent of the population of Europe, more than 70 per cent percent of the convictions for espionage occurred there.[82] Most eye opening, Estonia–with a population of merely 1.3 million–alone had more than 1/3 of all espionage convictions. This should not be interpreted as the Baltic countries being the main collection targets for Russia or China, however. That is arguably Brussels, at the heart of both EU and NATO decision-making, and surreptitiously identified as the 'espionage capital' of Europe.[83] But in Belgium, only a single conviction for espionage was identified, and several large European countries (the UK, France, Spain, and Italy) similarly had few or no convictions. This implies that the number of espionage convictions is not an appropriate metric for how prioritized a country is as a collection target, or of the espionage threat. Instead, it arguably indicates policy choices on how to best conduct counterintelligence (CI). And specifically, whether espionage cases should be publicly prosecuted, or more discreet methods pursued. Especially Estonia has long prosecuted suspected spies, with Latvia and Lithuania eventually adopting similar approaches.[84]

Given history and geography, Russia has ample recruitment opportunities amongst Russian-speakers in the Baltic countries, especially amongst those who still have relatives across the border, who are married to Russian citizens, have business interests in Russia, or amongst outspokenly pro-Russian politicians or activists. The region is also of strategic interest to the Kremlin, as one of the most likely site for a potential NATO-Russia conflict.[85] Part of the Baltic response has been to adopt up-to-date espionage legislation and local intelligence services have accumulated expertise on detecting and prosecuting spies. Lastly, there is a policy of prosecuting and publicising cases of espionage, including granting access to espionage convicts by international media.[86] This reflects a European policy-debate, underway in intelligence circles for at least a decade.[87] Over time, more European countries have seemingly concluded that the Estonian approach is the appropriate one.

Last but not least, convictions on espionage charges is also contingent on having up-to-date legislation, which is realistically applicable. Analyzing why there are so few convictions on espionage in Belgium, in spite of the concentration of intelligence officers in Brussels, outdated legislation has repeatedly been identified as one of the main culprits.[88] Beyond this, one expert on Belgian intelligence notes, "Let's be honest [...] A hostile operating environment is Moscow with the FSB. It's not Brussels with the Belgian State Security Service".[89] another piece of anecdotal evidence is provided by Latvia. In 2018, the deputy head of the Latvian Security Police argued that the main reasons that so few spies had previously been caught 'is due to the shortcomings in the legislation' (amended in 2016). Between 2010 and 2016, authorities launched six criminal probes 'which fizzled out due to the archaic legislation'.[90] Following legal amendments, at least three spies have been convicted. Other European countries, such as the Czech Republic, may face similar difficulties.[91] Conversely, a former Estonian prosecutor noted that the ability to bargain an agreement between the accused, the counsel and prosecutor has been key to the country's convictions of spies, with all Estonian espionage trials since 2007 ending in settlements.[92]

The differences between espionage against the US and Europe can largely be explained by geopolitical factors. That is, the dominance of Russian espionage cases is a consequence in part of Russia's geographical proximity, ease of recruitment, strong regional security interests and determination to exert influence, particularly in former Soviet Union republics, and amongst former members of the Warsaw Pact. This aligns well with Russia's overarching security- and defence policy.[93] But this legacy effect is also visible in who is recruited, insofar that many recruits were either dual or naturalized citizens, married to Russian citizens, had relatives or business ventures in Russia, or had served in the Soviet or Eastern Bloc security establishment before the end of the Cold War. Hence, in seeking to recreate a new, Cold War-type world order, Russia has largely drawn on the legacies of its predecessor.

Conversely, how European countries have responded to the threat corresponds closely with how they view Russia. The Baltic States and Poland – but more recently, also other northern European countries – have become very proactive in their counterintelligence operations, seeking to highlight the threat, and demonstrate their capability and will to resist it.[94] This likewise mirrors geopolitical outlooks, insofar that European countries that view Russia as its primary threat, have taken the strongest and most visible measures to counteract its espionage.[95] Other European countries, further removed from the Russian threat both geographically and mentally, may have been more reluctant to overtly confront Moscow. The war in Ukraine might change this, but the countries that feel most directly threatened by Russia will likely remain the most proactive in arresting and prosecuting Russian spies.

## Conclusion and Avenues for Future Research

This article provides a basis for beginning to fill the lacuna of comparative, cross-national research on espionage in Europe, in what could prove to be a both fruitful and timely new research field. As a first attempt, the study seeks to demonstrate that pursuing this line of research is inherently complex and time-consuming, but ultimately doable and worthwhile. The article provides us with an approximate sense of the universe of espionage cases in Europe over the past decade, including similarities and differences vis-à-vis contemporary espionage in the US. Some of these similarities may seem intuitive or self-evident, but until we compile comparable datasets, there is simply no way of knowing this with certainty. But the article also pinpoints a number of gaps in our knowledge. Hence, a first step in elaborating upon this article could involve expanding the sample, by i.a. adding recent cases[96] prolonging the timeline backwards, or adding more countries into the analysis.[97] A related avenue includes analyzing the identified cases from various perspectives, including for instance whether a typology for different categories of espionage can be developed, or analyzing changes in the frequency of espionage convictions over time. A number of different avenues of inquiry could also be pursued, including explaining the overrepresentation of male spies; analyzing whether civilian spies differ systematically from the military/intelligence moles; and exploring the wide divergence on convergence on convictions on espionage charges (particularly in regional powers), including through comparative legal studies.

Last but not least, the pantheon of 'paradigmatic cases' of espionage is to date dominated by Anglo-Saxon cases. They could however be complemented with at least a few of the most high-profile, contemporary cases from continental Europe. While far from complete, this could include a Deniss Metsavas,[98] an Austrian army officer,[99] a Portuguese counter intelligence officer,[100] Alexei Dressen,[101] and two Swedish-Iranian brothers (one of whom worked for Swedish intelligence and security agencies).[102] While international media have provided portraits of some of these spies, incisive case studies of the type previously devoted to US spies could improve our understanding of contemporary espionage decisively. Finally, comparative research on espionage in Europe is in its infancy, but there is a multitude of promising avenues for future research. And in pursuing them, intelligence scholars could both expand the empirical basis for this line of research, and elaborate some methodological approaches that have thus far been notably absent from the field.[103] As the Russo-Ukrainian war has set in motion what could well become a European 'decade of the spy', they could simultaneously also help us better understand the nature of the threat.

*Writer Michael Jonsson holds a Ph.D in political science from the Department of Government at Uppsala University and works as a Deputy Research Director at the Swedish Defense Research Agency (Sw. FOI). Dr. Jonsson has published i.a. with Survival, Studies in Conflict and Terrorism, European Security and Georgetown Journal of International Affairs. He is also the editor (with Svante Cornell) of Crime, Conflict and the State in Post-communist Eurasia (Pennsylvania University Press, 2014).*
*Journal information: Print ISSN: 0268-4527 Online ISSN: 1743-9019, 7 issues per year. Intelligence and National Security is covered by the following abstracting, indexing and citation services: ABC-CLIO - Historical Abstracts; ABC-CLIO - America: History and Life; World Political Science Abstracts; Historical Abstracts and America: life and history; CSA Political Science and Government and British Humantities Index; Lancaster Index to Defence; International Security Literature and Sociological Abstracts. Aims and scope: "The premier journal of intelligence studies" Eliot A. Cohen, Foreign Affairs. Intelligence has never played a more prominent role in international politics than it does now in the early years of the twenty-first century. National intelligence services are larger than ever, and they are more transparent in their activities in the policy making of democratic nations. Intelligence and National Security is widely regarded as the world's leading scholarly journal focused on the role of intelligence and secretive agencies in international relations. It examines this aspect of national security from a variety of perspectives and academic disciplines, with insightful articles research and written by leading experts based around the globe. Espionage by Europeans: treason and counterintelligence in post-Cold war Europe. Michael Jonsson. Received 07 Feb 2023, Accepted 23 Aug 2023, Published online: 11 Sep 2023. Intelligence and National Security. To cite this article: Michael Jonsson (11 Sep 2023): Espionage by Europeans: treason and counterintelligence in post-Cold war Europe, Intelligence and National Security, DOI:10.1080/026*

*84527.2023.2254020. © 2023 Swedish Defence Research Agency. Published by Informa UK Limited, trading as Taylor & Francis Group. Published online: 11 Sep 2023. Contact Michael Jonsson Michael.Jonsson@foi.se. IIntelligence and National Security. https://doi.org/10.1080/02684527.2023.2254020. © 2023 Swedish Defence Research Agency. Published by Informa UK Limited, trading as Taylor & Francis Group.*

Chapter 8

# Political Drivers of Muslim Youth Radicalisation in France: Religious Radicalism as a Response to Nativism

*Max-Valentin Robert & Ayhan Kaya*

## Abstract

A substantial amount of literature has developed around the individual determinants of radical political preferences. Widely used to study electoral support for far-right parties, this perspective has rarely been mobilised to understand the dynamics of radicalisation, or the process of going back to the 'roots', among fractions of Western Muslim youth involved in political Islam. To address this, 37 semi-structured interviews were conducted between 2020 and 2021 as part of ongoing ERC Advanced Grant research with young (aged 18–30) self-identifying Muslims of Turkish and Moroccan descent based in the Paris or Lyon areas. Also drawing on the social movements literature, we uncovered two sets of factors influencing radicalisation, each based on two distinct oppositional sets of attitudes: (1) a feeling of estrangement from mainstream societal values, such as morality, secularism, and a perceived assimilationist trend emanating from the French national frame, and (2) a sense of dissatisfaction towards the political-institutional system, which appeared as latent criticisms of the current state of representative democracy, distrust of political and media actors, and discontent towards the current French party system.

Keywords: Radicalisation, secularism, assimilation, securitisation, stigmatisation.

## Introduction

Much of the literature on radicalisation focuses on Islamist extremism and jihadist terrorism. Looking at the historical roots of radicalism, the subject is a relative one and has often been a force of progress. As such, its derivative, 'radicalisation' is not necessarily a synonym for violence or extremism (Bartlett and Miller Citation 2012; Schmid Citation 2013). The article proposes a distinction between non-violent and violent radicalisms. Policy-makers have also followed the same path that reduces radicalisation to violence and overlooks its non-violent, critical, relational, reactionary, and oppositional claims against the dominant regimes of representation that may frame some individuals and/or social groups in stereotypical and stigmatised ways. For instance, in response to the terrorist incidents that have occurred since 2014, France has developed and implemented several national plans to tackle and prevent violent radicalisation. The state's top-down approach has seen a raft of counter-radicalisation measures, coordinated at the central governmental and local prefectural levels. Three sets of measures have been taken: primary prevention to anticipate the risks of attack, secondary prevention to mitigate the risks from radicalised individuals, and tertiary prevention to monitor such individuals and prevent the recurrence of violent actions (Lahnait Citation2021).

However, this political framing failed to pinpoint the root causes of the radicalisation of self-identified Muslim youth who, we found, expressed two distinct oppositional sets of attitudes towards mainstream society. We identified these attitudes by reviewing prior research into social movements and conducting 37 semi-structured interviews with young (aged 18–30), self-identifying Muslims of Turkish and Moroccan origins living in the vicinity of either Paris or Lyon, before analysing the resulting data. The first oppositional attitude was a tendency for our interlocutors to distance themselves from mainstream societal values such as morality, secularism, and a perceived 'assimilationist' trend in the French national context. The second attitude was a feeling of dissatisfaction towards the political-institutional system, manifested as latent criticisms of the current state of representative democracy, distrust towards political and media actors, and discontent with the current French party system. If such perceptions towards the ongoing functioning of French democracy tend to be shared in other segments of the population outside Muslim and/or immigrant-origin groups – as was exemplified by the case of Yellow Vests (Guerra, Alexandre, and Gonthier Citation2020; Gonthier and Guerra Citation2022), we notice nonetheless a singularity within this part of the public opinion, who express specific grievances against what is generally interpreted as a hostile framing from the media, as well as a perceived process of securitisation directed against their religious community. Thus, the above-mentioned categorisation represents our efforts to specify the individual political determinants of non-violent reactionary radicalisation among self-identified Muslim youths – processes alienating and distancing them from the state and mainstream society.

Following the major methodological aspects, this article first explains how the French authorities have framed the issue of Islam through a securitising viewpoint (Della Porta Citation2014; Kaya Citation2015, Citation2009) over the last few years, and how this discourse has structured this reductionist approach. After reviewing recent literature on French Muslims, we describe the individualisation of religiosity among Western Muslim populations. We then detail how our interlocutors perceived their Muslim identities in a secularised and traditionally assimilationist context, and how they responded to the tone of public discussions on secularism and assimilation. Lastly, we describe our interlocutors' evaluations of representative democracy and how the mainstream media represents Muslims.

**Methodological approach**

A range of methods was used in this study, from desk research to discourse analysis (Fairclough Citation1992) of secondary sources as well as the primary data obtained from semi-structured interviews held with our young adult French Muslim participants. Using snowball sampling, all interviews were conducted between early 2020 and late 2021 by the corresponding author of this article, supervised by his co-author, during the ERC-funded PRIME Youth Project. Our two research fields were the regions of Paris and Lyon, two areas that are well-known for their historical Muslim and/or immigrant presence. A majority of our 37 interlocutors are descendants of Moroccan (n = 21: 12 women and nine men) and Turkish immigrants (n = 16: 9 women and seven men), while a minority experienced a migration trajectory themselves. However, all our interlocutors were French citizens and expressed in various ways a politicized view of their religion–a minority of them were, for instance, committed in organisations ideologically close to what is generally labeled as 'political Islam'.[1] The interview data were collected in two rounds of field research in 2020 and 2021. Reaching potential participants required the co-author to overcome two difficulties: the first was initial contact itself, in the context of the COVID-19 crisis and lockdown that was in effect during a part of our study's first year in 2020 (which consequently made necessary the conducting of the interviews through online and digital means). The second difficulty was for the co-author to integrate two groups from different cultural and religious backgrounds: the interviewer was neither a Muslim nor of Moroccan or Turkish origin – although his knowledge of the Turkish language and his life experiences in Turkey were sometimes helpful in building trust with especially some interlocutors of Turkish origin.

We opted to focus on the specific case of French citizens of Moroccan and Turkish origin due to the importance of these two diasporas' local presence: according to the data provided by INSEE (Institut national de la statistique et des études économiques–National Institute of Statistics and Economic Studies), respectively 802.000 and 251.000 immigrants living in France in 2019 originated from Morocco and Turkey. That same year, the number of Moroccan and Turkish immigrants' descendants living in France amounted to 964.000 and 313.000.[2] Furthermore, this choice was motivated by a common characteristic shared by the Turkish and Moroccan authorities towards their nationals living abroad: the use of religious diplomacy as a policy tool mobilised to manage their Diasporas (Kaya and Drhimeur Citation2022). Nevertheless, we also considered it relevant to compare two countries that do not have the same historical relationship with France: while Morocco was a French protectorate that became independent in 1956, Turkey has never suffered a past status as a colonised country (Haynes Citation 2021).

## A Reductionist Approach: Securitising Islam

This article argues that French state actors have failed to respond to the rise of radicalisation among self-identified Muslim youngsters, partly because they cannot distinguish between radicalism[3] and extremism.[4] In this article, we use the term, 'radical', in a different way from its conventional use in the contemporary world since the September 11 terrorist attacks in New York. We use the term to refute the reductionist understandings that have become prevalent in policy-making processes, media, and even social sciences. We claim that such understandings are likely to postulate radical positionalities as threats to democracy. Referring to our self-identified young Muslim interlocutors' first-hand testimonies, beliefs, narratives, reasons, desires, goals, and religiosity, we argue the other way around and present them as different manifestations of struggle for democracy. Some young people become increasingly angry and radicalised due to various root causes such as socioeconomic, political, spatial, psychological, and nostalgic forms of deprivation that have become more recurrent in the age of globalisation. In the aftermath of September 11, the term radicalisation became intertwined with 'recruitment' by extremists, who try to persuade 'angry individuals' (Gurr Citation1969) to join their war (Coolsaet Citation2019). Nonetheless, it is obvious that there is an emerging scientific need to emphasise that being radical in socioeconomic, political, philosophical, ethno-cultural, religious, and ideational terms should not be necessarily translated into violent extremism and terrorism, and can also be interpreted as potential struggles for the deepening of democracy.

The term 'radical' has become 'floating' (Lévi Straus Citation1987), or 'empty signifier' (Laclau and Mouffe Citation1985), that is to say, words that might not necessarily refer specifically to something existing in the real world. What is remarkable is the way in which the term 'radicalisation' has been through since the 19th century, especially since the 1970s. For instance, in the 1960s and 70s, the term 'radical' was the label given by violent organizations to those groups who occupied the middle ground between violent and non-violent methods. In those days, the experts' discourse tended to be more nuanced in using different terms to explain various phenomena. The TREVI group,[5] for instance, was created in 1976 and named ten years after by an acronym that specifically distinguished Terrorism, Radicalism, Extremism, Violence, and Internationalism (Fadil and Koning Citation2019, 4).

Since September 11, the term 'radicalisation' has been used interchangeably with 'extremism', 'terrorism', 'fundamentalism', and 'violence' in media and political discourse. Indeed, radicalisation research originally arose from the need to organise the discourse and acts of public authorities (Marchal and Ahmed Salem Citation2018; Coolsaet 2029; Kaya and Bee in this Issue; Peels in this Issue). The discourse of politicians and experts in Western countries reveals a conception of radicalisation that is mostly individual, and (almost-exclusively) Islamist (Maskaliunaite Citation 2015; Coolsaet Citation 2019). Most institutional and political radicalisation interventions are deeply rooted in psychological and religious considerations but exclude the structural analysis that might illuminate other aspects of this complex issue.

One problematic aspect of radicalisation, as used in public discourse, is its apparent use to legitimise and reinforce previously established systems of securitisation and police repression of migrant heritage populations (Rigouste Citation2012). However, paradoxically, this conception of radicalisation (whose sources tend to be limited–in mainstream public discourse – to religious and migration-related factors) has often been described as potentially fuelling radicalisation among the very same deprived social groups. Indeed, in an atmosphere marked by stigmatisation and alienation, the members of these groups may be driven towards more radical attitudes (e.g. increased prejudice against native populations) through increased feelings of disconnection from society in general, as well as socioeconomic, political, spatial and psychological deprivation (Gurr Citation1969; Doosje, Loseman, and Van Den Bos Citation2013).

Social Movements Theory provides us with a few conceptualisations to understand how stigmatised and alienated young Muslims in France and elsewhere in Europe become radicalised through socioeconomic and political forms of deprivation as well as feelings of disconnection from society in general. Donatella Della Porta's (Citation2018) notion of 'relational radicalisation' develops within the contentious politics paradigm, that is, individuals generate their socio-political positions in relation to how they are treated by others as the members of society in general and/or state actors. According to Charles Tilly (Citation2003, 5), scholars working on political radicalisation can be categorized as 'idea people', who look at ideologies; 'behaviour people', who stress human heritage; or 'relational people', who make transactions among persons and groups much more central than do idea or behaviour people. In this regard, relational perspective focuses on interpersonal processes that promote, inhibit, or channel violent and/or non-violent politics (Tilly Citation2003). In other words, radicalisation follows a gradual process, defined as actions of some kind associated with other actions and reactions, often expressed in some kind of dialogical, dialectical and reciprocal relationship (Della Porta Citation2018).

This line of thinking is also reciprocated by Craig Calhoun (Citation2011) who made a three-fold classification of radicalism: philosophical radicalism, tactical radicalism and reactionary radicalism. Accordingly, philosophical radicalism of theorists was about penetrating the roots of society with rational and analytical programs to understand the structural transformation of the public sphere. Tactical radicalism of activists was mainly about their search for immediate change that required violence and other extreme actions to achieve it. Finally, reactionary radicalism of those suffering from the destabilising effects of modernization and globalisation was more about their quest for saving what they valued in communities and cultural traditions from eradication by capitalism (Calhoun Citation2011). Young Muslims in France, at least our interlocutors, have demonstrated that they have become more associated with Islamic values and thought as a response to the ways in which majority society and the state have stereotypically framed Islam and Muslims in general.

What one could see here is a relational and reactionary form of radicalisation that is the symptom of increased feelings of disconnection from society resulting from the prevalence of anti-Muslim racism as well as socioeconomic, political, spatial and psychological deprivation. Our working definition of reactionary radicalism is that it is a backward-looking political orientation characterised by anti-stances and dogmatic thinking associated with values of security, tradition and aversion to stimulation and new experiences that foster intolerance towards out-groups (Capelos and Katsanidou Citation2018; Capelos and Demertzis Citation2018). Relational and reactionary forms of radicalism are expressed by young self-identified Muslims in France through what their 'cultural repertoire' (Tilly Citation1978) offers them. In the case of Muslim youth, cultural repertoire might include religion, ethnicity, culture, tradition, heritage, past, and patriarchy, depending on the country of origin.

The feelings of disconnection from society as well as socioeconomic and political deprivation, as mentioned before, are known predictors of ethno-cultural and religious radicalisation and essentialism: indeed, radicalism sometimes operates as a tactic (De Certeau Citation1984) used by individuals to restore significance to their lives and a feeling of personal control after experiencing various ambiguities, instabilities, and insecurities (Tilly Citation1978; Kay et al. Citation2010). Ethno-cultural and religious resurgence may be interpreted as a symptom of existing structural social, economic, political and psychological problems such as unemployment, racism, xenophobia, exclusion, assimilation, alienation, and anomie. Scientific data uncover that migrant-origin groups tend to affiliate themselves with politics of identity, ethnicity, religiosity, and sometimes violence in order to tackle such structural constraints and dominant regimes of representation (Clifford Citation1987; Gilroy et al. Citation1995). This is actually a form of politics initiated by outsider groups as opposed to the kind of politics generated by 'those within' as Alistair MacIntyre (Citation1971) decoded much earlier. According to MacIntyre (Citation1971) there are two forms of politics: politics of those within and politics of those excluded. Those within tend to employ legitimate political institutions (parliament, political parties, the media) in pursuing their goals, and those excluded resort to honour, culture, ethnicity, religion, roots and tradition in doing the same.

It should be noted here that MacIntyre does not place culture and religion in the private space; they are rather inherently located in the public space. Therefore, the main motive behind the development of ethno-cultural and religious essentialism by migrant and minority groups may be perceived as a concern to be attached to the political-public sphere. It is then unsurprising for individuals with a gloomy outlook on the present and the future, who are exposed to anti-Muslim racism and intersectional forms of discrimination in everyday life to resort to heritage, honour, religion, ethnicity, language, tradition and myths, all of which they believe cannot be pried from their hands, and to define themselves in those terms (Eliade Citation1991; Clifford Citation1994). To that effect, we want to use the very literal meanings of the terms 'radical' and 'radicalisation' in this work. The word 'radical' comes from the Latin word 'radix' (root), and the term 'radicalisation' then literally means the process of 'going back to the roots' (Calhoun Citation2011).

Essentialising conceptions of specific social groups such as youth who identify as Muslim often carry harmful sociopolitical consequences (McDonald Citation2011; Brown and Saeed Citation2015; Coolsaet Citation2019). Neoliberal governance coupled with the securitisation of Islam might paradoxically be used to culturalise (or 'religionise') the consequences of policy decisions, masking their socioeconomic and political underpinnings (Kaya Citation2015; Kaya and Adam-Troian Citation2021). This may fuel socio-political tensions and trigger threat perception processes among migrant-origin minorities and majority societies, causing co-radicalisation among self-identifying Muslims and the nativist segments of majority societies (Kaya and Adam-Troian Citation2021; Kaya Citation2021). When neoliberalism conceals the structural causes of radicalisation, countermeasures are reduced to security-related policing responses. Accordingly, the neoliberal parties' response to radicalisation has been to implement cautionary policing measures (Della Porta Citation2014). This redoubled sense of threat could lead to radicalisation – and even extremisation – among some deprived social groups, such as ethnocultural minorities (Orehek and Vazeou-Nieuwenhuis Citation2014).

## Current Research on Muslims in France

Sociological research examining the religiosity of immigrant-origin French Muslims notes their higher levels of religious commitment compared with the majority population (Galland Citation2019), which is becoming increasingly secularised (Dargent Citation2019). Furthermore, the religiosity gap between younger generations from Christian and Muslim backgrounds seems to be widening (Tiberj Citation 2020). Thus, while French Muslims appear to be maintaining their beliefs, the religious identity of their Christian counterparts is becoming increasingly culturalised (Brubaker Citation2017). These differentiated relationships to religion illuminate the specificities of Muslim public opinion in France, which views moral liberalism less favourably than the overall population (Galland Citation2019). The greater conservatism of Western Muslim values compared to the social majority has been confirmed by research from other countries. This conservatism is usually more pronounced around issues linked to sexual morals and gender roles (Beekers and Schrijvers Citation 2020). However, in the French case, the moral conservatism of Muslim citizens does not translate into electoral support for right-wing parties, with parties of the left supported far more widely (Brouard and Tiberj Citation2005). This phenomenon is reported elsewhere in case studies on Muslim populations of other Western countries (Azabar and Thijssen Citation 2020).

Moreover, ideological divergences from the majority do not imply that European Muslims were more inclined to take up protest activities. For example, Hadjar et al. found that the level of religious practice among young Muslims in Germany did not correlate with their justifications for violent activism, which were influenced by other socioeconomic and political factors (Hadjar et al. Citation 2019). Likewise, in Denmark and Sweden, the main factor in Muslim endorsement of violent protest was the phenomenon of meta-cultural threat or 'victimization-by-proxy' (Obaidi et al. Citation 2018), rather than levels of religious observance. A pan-European study, however, noted that levels of religious activity and justifications for terrorism were strongly associated (Egger and Magni-Berton Citation 2021).

In his comparative study of the public incorporation of Muslim immigrants in Britain, France, and Germany between 1973 and 2001, Koenig (Citation2005) showed how integration followed specific patterns shaped by the legally institutionalised logic of traditional religious politics that emerged from historically specific trajectories of state formation and nation-building. A first crucial factor is a degree to which the idea of the 'individual' in each polity is institutionalised since this affects how 'religion' itself is defined. In corporatist polities, where rights are ascribed to corporate bodies, religion is regarded as a formal membership organisation that can be incorporated directly into the state's rationalising project. However, in statist and liberal policies, where the individual is the primary bearer of rights, 'religion' is perceived as an individual orientation organised via voluntary associations. A second factor is the degree of 'stateness': in nation-states oriented toward statist or corporatist polity models, such as France, Germany, and the Netherlands, the incorporation of Muslim minorities is coordinated by the state, while in liberal polities, such as Great Britain, it takes the form of civil negotiations, mostly at the local level (Koenig Citation2005). The third factor is the relationship of national symbols to the metanarratives of 'secularisation'. Universalistic symbols of national identity may be linked to ideologies of secularism, such as French laïcité (state secularism). In these cases, explicitly religious claims for recognition are conceived as transgressing the symbolic boundary between the 'religious' and the 'secular' (Zolberg Citation2004).

## Beyond Essentialisation: The Growing Individualisation of Islam by Young Western Muslims

Previous research suggests that French Muslims increasingly support the public visibility of religiosity while expressing latent criticism of the idea of a 'neutral' public space (Del Grosso Citation2015; Villechaise and Bucaille Citation2020). Nevertheless, such demands for greater expressive possibilities among Muslims are not only directed 'against' the political frame and the dominant cultural referential: case studies of other Western Muslim populations have shown that more individualized readings of Islam may also be mobilised in a discourse of disruption directed at practices inherited from their families and/or communities of origin (O'Brien Citation2018). Consequently, the youngest Muslim generations may articulate an emerging dichotomy between what they consider as 'cultural' Islam on the one hand and 'pure/true' Islam (Ali Citation2018) on the other. This individualisation of the relationship to Islam (Kaya Citation2009, 184) and the self-empowerment linked to inherited traditions are often part of a process of self-learning (Seurat Citation2020), and are particularly mobilised by young Muslim women as a tool of enfranchisement from family standards (Kaya Citation2009, 187). The Islamic allegiance of these youths could also be interpreted as a quest for emancipation from the parental culture (Kaya Citation2009, 186). For converts to Salafism, the legitimisation conferred by religious knowledge is combined with the search for moral superiority over the family environment (Zegnani Citation2018).

These strands of religious individualisation are redefining the very meaning of faith in a personalized form that challenges older definitions in which religion and culture are not distinguished (Kaya Citation2009: 192–193). In this context, such acts of opposition may be interpreted as expressing the need to belong to a legitimate counter-hegemonic global discourse such as that of Islam, from which symbolic power is derived (Kaya Citation2009, 180). Identifying with counter-hegemonic global discourses may be associated with processes of transnational identification, as highlighted in some studies of Muslim populations in various Western countries (Edmunds Citation2010), and may be linked to specific forms and drivers of social identification (Kranendonk, Vermeulen, and van Heelsum Citation2018), and dual identities (Cardenas Citation2019).

A significant body of work has questioned the 'identity crises' supposedly experienced by Westerners with Muslim backgrounds (Kabir Citation2012; Ali Citation2018). Some of this work underlines the dynamics of Muslim integration into the majority society (Beaman Citation2017; Manning and Akhtar Citation2020) while other researchers investigate how this new generation has forged a distinct popular culture (Kabir Citation2012; Nilan Citation2017; Ali Citation2018; O'Brien Citation2018). The individualisation of identity assertion has frequently been highlighted (Kaya Citation2012), as well as how young Muslim Westerners have negotiated their integration into the host society (Frisina Citation2010). However, in spite of this negotiated integration, the conclusions of empirical research into national identification tend to concur that religious and/or ethnic identifications may weaken the sense of national belonging expressed by members of Muslim diasporic communities in Western countries (Verkuyten and Yildiz Citation2007; Bisin et al. Citation2008). This distancing from national identity may be a reaction to what is perceived as a spreading securitisation discourse produced by political and media representations of migration and Islam (Calhoun, Citation2011; Kaya Citation2012). This is what Craig Calhoun (Citation2011) calls reactionary radicalism, a stance developed by young pious Muslim youths to refute the essentialist and orientalist approach that perceives Islam with a single outlook, a stance that does not recognise the plurality of outlooks in Islam (Ciftci, Wuthrich, and Shamaileh Citation2022, 197–199).

Research on Islamophobia points to the common misperceptions about Islam or Muslims as the root cause of anti-Muslim sentiment in the West (Allen Citation2010; Halliday Citation1999; Ciftci, Wuthrich, and Shamaileh Citation2022). The assumption underlying such perceptions reduces Islam to a uniform and homogenous faith, or in other words, pious Muslims to single-minded actors or agents irrespective of their ethno-cultural, societal, educational, gendered, and historical differences (Ciftci, Wuthrich, and Shamaileh Citation2022). The failure of multicultural policies in Western European democracies to facilitate the integration of Muslim-origin people and reduce social tensions, usually results from the misleading assumption that all Muslims conform to a single outlook and that Muslim religiosity leads to uniform attitudes and behaviour (Ciftci, Wuthrich, and Shamaileh Citation2022, 199). Our selection of both Moroccan and Turkish-origin Muslim youths is also a conscious choice to challenge the conventional wisdom in European societies that portrays Islam as a uniform religion. Some of our interlocutors rather depicted Islam as a phenomenon with diverse implications, practices, conventions, and traditions grounded in historical, social, and local contexts (Ahmed Citation2017).

## Estrangement from Mainstream Values

### Being a traditionalist minority in a secularised society

Vincent Tiberj (Citation2020) noticed that in the French Muslim population, frequent mosque attendance was associated with more traditionalist views on gender relations, women's sexuality, and homosexuality. Within our sample of youngsters of Moroccan and Turkish descent, morality was indeed a core factor in their estrangement from the mainstream French society, with their values differing from those of the majority. This discrepancy was exemplified by the following remarks from a 22-year-old French-Moroccan female student: Due to your religion, you're often in a confrontation with an environment that goes against what you are. So as not to hide anything from you, and to speak bluntly, when you are in a business school, what do you see? It drinks, it fucks, it smokes – things that are all prohibited by Islam. So, at first, I couldn't find my place. When you're a Muslim, you find yourself in an ecosystem where you question yourself, which sometimes clashes with your deep values. (22, F, Moroccan origin, Paris area, 27.08.2020).

This attachment to traditional values was often expressed when our interlocutors described their general social environment, such as non-Muslim friendly circles. A 23-year-old French-Turkish man stated the following when asked about his friendships: However, with my friends, we talk about it a lot more. And there, people are divided into two groups: there are my Turkish friends – and with them, we think the same – and my French friends – whom we never really agree with. With my French friends, we never have the same ideas, especially when it comes to religion and culture. And politically, I am more conservative than they are. As for them, they're not conservative at all (23, M, Turkish origin, Lyon area, 31.05.2020). Independent from their social relationships, many of our interlocutors seemed disturbed by what they viewed as a trend towards greater moral and sexual liberalism. The divergence between their ideals and a perceived wider rise in progressivism was encapsulated by the following statements from a 30-year-old male teacher of Moroccan origin: There are also a lot of gay-friendly bars [in Paris]: as far as this population is concerned, Parisians have a very favourable view. They have not a neutral, but a positive view. I even think it's frowned upon to be heterosexual, in Paris … (30, M, Moroccan origin, Paris area, 16.11.2021).

The latent rejection of cultural liberalism also manifested itself through negative judgements of the ongoing evolution of the French Muslim community, centring on what is interpreted as increasing secularisation among young people who identify as Muslims: For example, I once got angry with an old North-African friend because I told her that the way she dressed was not worthy of a good Muslim. I told her it'd be better for her if she dressed more modestly. That provoked an argument between us, and since then we haven't spoken to each other (23, M, Turkish origin, Lyon area, 31.05.2020). This perceived gap in moral values was most expressed – particularly by females – concerning gender issues, differentiating them from the members of majority society. Indeed, Fabien Truong noticed the prevalence of clear gender-related social roles in the specific case of the suburban Muslim youth – through hints of what 'real men' and 'real women' should be like (Truong Citation2017). Some testimonies from the interviews illustrated how speakers had internalised the 'knowing-how-to-behave' discourse, especially in a family context:

For example, as a girl, I know that I shouldn't talk too much with the boys in high school. It's something that's improper, that's inappropriate. And it's the same at home: in Islam, you should have a certain posture in front of your parents. For instance, when a grown-up comes into a room and you're there, you shouldn't lie down, but you should sit down (18, F, Turkish origin, Lyon area, 08.03.2021). Such gender-based moral positioning occasionally aroused incomprehension from members of the social majority. Thus, female interlocutors might mention past experiences of difficult conversations on topics related to feminism or women's rights, such as this 25-year-old interlocutor, who wore a headscarf: One day I was waiting at the tram station, and a woman, who was probably of North African descent, yelled at me: "Our mothers fought against this". Sometimes you can even get insults too, in a gratuitous way. [...] Sometimes people comfort you like you're sick, or sometimes they remind you of things like, "This is old, this is archaic: you have to evolve now". For example, a friend's mom is a feminist, and she told me once that I should take it off because symbolically it's violent for her. It's like an aggressive act to her, she told me. She also told me that it's a sign of submission to men. From her viewpoint, it is a symbol of oppression. I can understand her vision, but I live very well with the fact of being veiled (25, F, Moroccan origin, Lyon area, 24.03.2021).

The young people we interviewed thus expressed their estrangement from the values of mainstream society. This moral differentiation shaped various aspects of their identities: their perception that they were out of step with the majority and their sense of extraneousness in the social environment, which could occasionally generate mutual misunderstanding during everyday interactions. Furthermore, several youngsters criticised what they perceived as the growth of cultural liberalism which they also claimed to have witnessed within the French Muslim community itself. Independent of this social criticism, this point of view also surfaced in their interpretations of the political-institutional framing of religion-state relationships and descriptions of French-style laïcité.

## Young Muslims and French-style laïcité

On 15 March 2004, a law was passed restricting the use of religious symbols in public schools,[6] while public use of the full-face veil (niqab) was banned from all public spaces after 11 October 2010.[7] These successive restrictions have been viewed with suspicion by French Muslims, particularly because the headscarf issue is widely featured in French media and political debates. For example, the recent authorisation of the burkini in the public swimming pools of Grenoble has caused controversy among French politicians, with a dispute between the city's ecologist mayor (Eric Piolle) and the conservative president of the Auvergne-Rhône-Alpes region (Laurent Wauquiez) breaking out in May 2022.[8] Furthermore, in her 2022 presidential platform, Marine Le Pen even suggested fining Muslim women wearing headscarves in public areas. French-style secularism (laïcité) is somewhat maligned by the French-Muslim population, which would prefer the authorities to turn a blind eye to public expressions of religiosity. The following discussion with a 21-year-old student of Moroccan origin demonstrates this widespread perception:

120

Theoretically, [laïcité] is a divide between the state and religion, and religions can live and express themselves freely. Today, we are told that no religion should exist publicly in France. But religions raise human and universal questions. I think that religion should be more visible in society and at school – but it's currently taking a back seat. For example, the headscarf cannot be worn in public. We are facing a modified version of laïcité. The headscarf is interpreted as a sign of radicalisation, of subjugation. But if we make religion more visible at school, if we develop exchanges with religious communities, it will be obvious that veiled women should be seen in public (21, M, Moroccan origin, Lyon area, 18.05.2020). However, several interlocutors spontaneously recounted experiences of conflict with non-Muslim people regarding external manifestations of religiosity. These narratives mostly focused on headscarf-related issues, and illustrated an area of misunderstanding between the majority population and the Muslim minority. When our interlocutors tried to identify possible reasons for these latent tensions around visible religiosity, many alluded to the terrorist attacks which had recently shaken French society. Indeed, the following extracts indicate that these events contributed to the public affirmation of anti-Muslim resentment:

I don't like the way laïcité is defined today. The state tends to harden itself against Islam, from my viewpoint. But at the same time, we must remember all the tragic events that have happened to us. Since the terrorist attacks, everything has changed. We are not in the same context today. So even if the way that laïcité is presented today deeply annoys me, I can understand why we are in this situation now, because of all that has happened (27, F, Moroccan origin, Lyon area, 24.02.2021). Beyond institutional measures and daily interactions with the social majority, some of our interlocutors were apprehensive of the threat that secularisation posed to their cultural identity. This latent fear was apparent in the following remarks from a 25-year-old French-Moroccan interlocutor: Yet I feel good in France, and I feel at home, but I don't feel French. Being French, for me, is associated with … I know it's weird, but for me, being French means eating pork and drinking alcohol, and I can't accept that, because of my religion (25, F, Moroccan origin, Lyon area, 24.03.2021).

Similar rejections of assimilation distanced our participants from the social majority. The above-mentioned rejection encapsulates our participants' widespread distrust of French-style laïcité, which they viewed as a potential tool of cultural assimilation. In a similar vein, our interlocutors saw laïcité's attempt to make the public sphere 'neutral' as opposing public expressions of religiosity. Yet beyond such legal and political aspects, several interlocutors mentioned disagreements with non-Muslims on visible aspects of their religiosity–especially headscarf-wearing. In addition, most highlighted how terrorist attacks had tarnished the majority's image of Muslims and contributed to frame Islam as a problem in mainstream political discourse. Overall, our interlocutors rejected the dominant discourse of laïcité as they thought it was rather an assimilationist and politically motivated ideology imposing the majority society's moral codes on the Muslims.

## No to Assimilation, Yes to Integration

According to Roché, Astor, and Bilen (Citation2020), devout French Muslim teenagers tend to express lesser levels of national identification than irreligious ones. These findings echo some observations raised by our sample: among the Muslims of Moroccan and Turkish descent we interviewed, religious practice and assimilation to the 'national' culture were strongly and negatively correlated: nobody could assimilate into French society without shedding their Muslim identity. Faced with what is perceived as a latent assimilationist injunction from the mainstream society, Islam can, therefore, be relationally mobilised through three functionalities: as a 'guarantee of loyalty', a 'certification of singularity', and a 'floating political imagery' (Truong Citation2017, 120). This perceived incompatibility between being a practising Muslim and being 'fully French' is exemplified by the following remarks: I wouldn't be the person I am today if I weren't Muslim. I'd still be integrated into France, but because of my religion, I'd never be assimilated into French culture because I can't do everything the French do. There are things I can't eat and drink, for example (28, F, Turkish origin, Lyon area, 06.05.2021).

Although most participants rejected the authoritarian and homogenising nature of assimilation, they regarded integration as a fundamental part of adapting to the host society. This distinction between the two notions was explicitly mentioned by several interlocutors: Assimilation means no longer practicing one's culture, and no longer speaking one's language. It is when you live like a French person. I'm against it because I think you lose your identity when you assimilate. As a Turk and a Muslim, I want to keep some deep values and a particular way of living. And I want to pass these on to my children. Integration is something different: it's keeping your language, your religion, and your culture, but integrating into French society (22, M, Turkish origin, Lyon area, 12.09.2020).

Thus, several members of our Muslim sample clearly distinguished between assimilation and integration. The former was interpreted as an existential cultural threat, while the latter was perceived as a necessity. Many interlocutors also expressed their views on the accusation of 'communautarisme' (communitarianism) often made by right-wing political actors against the Muslim population. Without necessarily denying this phenomenon (and even while deploring it), most of our interlocutors interpreted it as a hidden racism emanating from conservative and/or nativist politicians: Today, Muslims are criticized for not mixing with French society: but if mixing means abandoning one's religion and culture, then it is normal that Muslims refuse this. But if we aren't asked to erase our identity, I don't understand why mixing would be impossible. [...] But the mixing must be done naturally: it must not be imposed by the state (27, F, Moroccan origin, Lyon area, 24.02.2021).

Thus, our sample of young Muslim people largely rejected assimilation, which they viewed as a harmful and unattainable policy objective, both due to religious strictures on behaviour and the latent association of 'Frenchness' with secularisation, as expressed in the declarations of several interlocutors. Faced with what is interpreted as a latent assimilationist injunction from the mainstream society, claiming their immigrant-origin and/or Muslim identity can be interpreted as the wish to mobilise 'the about-face gesture and the breakup show' (Truong Citation2017, 167). As a response to this perceived pressure, Islam can therefore be relationally mobilised through three functionalities: as a 'guarantee of loyalty', a 'certification of singularity', and a 'floating political imagery' (Truong Citation2017, 120). However, growing levels of religiosity and piety among our interlocutors do not necessarily mean that their religious identity becomes an impediment before their civic identity. On the contrary, our findings also reveal that our interlocutors have a general tendency to underline their Frenchness when asked about their value orientation. Besides, several scientific research also demonstrate that absolute levels of piety are generally associated with higher rather than lower levels of support for democracy (Ciftci, Wuthrich, and Shamaileh Citation2022).

Yet despite their outright rejection of assimilation, many of our interlocutors valued integration as an achievable (and desirable) goal and a 'third way' that could make their faith compatible with their respect for civic values. Furthermore, the reproach of 'communitarianism' is widely understood as a discursive tool used by political and media actors to stigmatise Islam and exclude the Muslim population. This blame exemplified a broader and more prevalent critical stance against the media-political sphere within our sample of French Muslims.

## Distrust towards representative democracy and the media: An unsatisfactory institutional system, a frustrating political offer

Western Muslims tend to trust public institutions independently of their political behaviour (Maxwell Citation2010) and their level of religiosity (Doerschler and Irving Jackson Citation2012). However, many of our French-Muslim interlocutors maintained a certain scepticism towards the current functioning of representative democracy: while only a minority rejected the democratic model outright, most of our interlocutors deplored how the model is currently enforced, viewing it as unsatisfactory and inadequate. For instance, several interlocutors were sceptical about voting and whether elected officials could implement actions that would impart concrete effects on their daily lives: We have the right to vote, and that's a very good thing. It's an important right. But whomever we vote for, do they have any real power? Can we really change things by voting, or isn't everything already decided beforehand? I don't know, but I'm sceptical that we're the ones who really decide. [...] Anyway, to give you an answer, I'd say "yes and no": voting changes some things. But it doesn't change life at all (28, F, Turkish origin, Lyon area, 06.05.2021).

The political ideology that the Muslim young people alluded to most frequently in the interviews – as a source of concern–was that of the radical right. Indeed, the anti-immigration stance of Marine Le Pen's National Rally (Rassemblement national–RN) and Eric Zemmour's Reconquest (Reconquête) was considered an outright threat by these young citizens. Additionally, the growing politicisation of Islam by the Western far-right (Berntzen Citation2020) tends to accentuate this concern within local Muslim minorities, and explains why our interlocutors rejected Marine Le Pen's party: I think the RN programme would accentuate inequalities based on origin because they defend a Zemmourian[9] vision of French society. They want everyone to have a French first name, for example.[...] Their dogma is to francise everyone. They are strongly Islamophobic, too (22, M, Turkish origin, Lyon area, 12.09.2020).

Our young Moroccan and Turkish-heritage interlocutors appeared more determined to reject the far-right which was featuring more prominently in political debates. Many participants justified their voting decisions in terms of blocking the RN from accessing power. This political objective, indeed, was often described as the main determinant of their voting choice.

While our interlocutors mentioned supporting Emmanuel Macron in the runoff against Marine Le Pen in the 2017 presidential election, they also criticized him heavily. Many accused Macron of moving away from the pro-multiculturalism and pro-immigration centrist discourse he had espoused in his 2017 campaign. They emphasised that a clear discursive shift away from this had occurred in the areas of Islam, migration, and diversity during Macron's first term. For example, this French-Moroccan participant mentioned the controversy around 'Islamo-leftism' ('islamo-gauchisme') initiated by some ministers and Macronist political figures against what they presented as academic 'complacency' towards Islamist activism.[10]

I think Macron kind of betrayed what he said during his 2017 campaign. [In] The Republic on the Move, they were saying they were neither left nor right, even though, in my opinion, they had a more left-wing discourse during the elections. And so, a lot of left-wing people voted for them, including me. But now, this party talks about Islamo-leftism, these kinds of things… They are far from the ideas they advocated during the campaign. And then, it's so ridiculous, this polemic around Islamo-leftism: it doesn't exist, and it's stigmatising to talk like that. It's a discourse of exclusion (26, F, Moroccan origin, Paris, area, 03.03.2021).

Another trope that occasionally occurred in some interviews was dissatisfaction with the General Security Law (Loi sécurité globale), enacted during Macron's first term: several participants seemed to interpret this measure as particularly targeting the Muslim population, and as contributing to what could be described as a 'suspicion of the uprising' (Truong Citation2017). Indeed, aside from issues linked to multiculturalism, some of our interlocutors also referred to the law's security implications, presented as securitarian and repressive: The last time I demonstrated was against the Global Security Law. This law is to the detriment of Black youngsters, Arab youngsters, or youngsters of other origins. It's going to make racial profiling worse (27, F, Moroccan origin, Lyon area, 17.02.2021). Lastly, after Samuel Paty (a teacher who had shown Charlie Hebdo's caricatures of the prophet Muhammed to his pupils, during a course on free speech) was assassinated by a radical Islamist, Emmanuel Macron's reaction was interpreted as a provocation by some of our interlocutors.[11] Indeed, his statements on free speech and the right to blaspheme were sometimes described as an attempt to stoke Islamophobia, as the following statements from a 27-year-old French-Moroccan woman exemplify:

Macron has done other uncool things, as well: for example, when the professor–may he rest in peace – was killed, Macron's reaction was to say: "We have the right to make fun of Islam, and we have to do it". For me, attacking my religion is unacceptable. (27, F, Moroccan origin, Lyon area, 17.02.2021). Most participants expressed scepticism about the ability of politicians to improve their situation, and their doubts about voting were an important theme within the sample. Our Muslim interlocutors described themselves as deeply opposed to radical right parties due to their anti-Islam stance and hostility towards immigration. Some also remarked – more or less explicitly – that Emmanuel Macron and The Republic on the Move had deceived them by shifting to the right on cultural issues. This critical stance extended to the media, particularly to journalistic framings of Islam.

## A weapon of mass stigmatisation? French Muslims' perceptions of the media

The widespread resentment of Western Muslim minorities towards the mainstream media in the US and several European countries has been widely reported (Kaya Citation2012). This latent distrust may constitute a reaction to its perceived essentialist and orientalist framing of Islam. In the US, for instance, Powell (Citation2018) showed how the media coverage of attacks committed by Muslim and non-Muslim terrorists contrasted. Similar tendencies appear to have manifested themselves in France (Deltombe Citation2007). As expected, our young French-Turkish and French-Moroccan interlocutors were often critical of the media, which they viewed as spreading negative images of Islam and Muslims: There have been events that have made headlines in the media, such as the terrorist attacks. The riots in the suburbs, too: this event finally turned against youngsters of immigrant origin. And then, all the problems in Syria, Afghanistan, or Iraq, degraded the image of Arabs and Muslims (27, F, Moroccan origin, Lyon area, 24.02.2021).

More specifically, French media attitudes were perceived as setting an anti-immigration and anti-Islamic agenda, fomenting racism and intolerance in society. The following statements exemplify this frequent reproach: It's not very fashionable to be a rebeu,[12] these days. Just listen to the media, these days. Just listen CNews[13]…We are not very well seen, with all these polemics… (24, M, Moroccan origin, Lyon area, 03-04-2021). Many of our Muslim interlocutors expressed distrust of the mainstream media and had consequently shifted to the social media, which some found a supposedly more reliable source of information: I like to use Twitter because they are faster in terms of news: they have more information in real-time, it's less censored. Compared to the TV, it's freer. The French media often distort reality. They put on TV what they want, we know that. They distort certain things, like on Muslims. It's the opposite on Twitter, where the points of view are more diverse, where there is less distortion. (21, M, Turkish origin, Paris area, 12.09.2020). While holding generally negative views of French politics, the interlocutors were even more critical of what they viewed as the dominant media discourse. Indeed, many described this discourse as hostile to Islam and marked by nativist stances, which explained why they had turned to social media as an alternative source of information. Yet despite the perceived rise of anti-Muslim sentiment in the mainstream media, the majority of participants explained that this agenda-setting did not visibly harm their everyday social interactions with their non-Muslim fellow citizens. Several of our interlocutors stated that their daily relations with the majority population remained peaceful, although mutual misunderstandings of the visible aspects of religiosity remained an issue, as mentioned previously.

## Conclusion

The qualitative research presented in this article has provided insight into how young Turkish- and Moroccan-origin French Muslims experience their religiosity in everyday life. It highlights the estrangement of young French Muslim people from the cultural norms of the social majority in terms of moral liberalism, secularisation, and gender roles. Our interlocutors opposed both French-style secularism and assimilation by perceiving the former as a road to the latter. Indeed, laïcité was often interpreted as an official quest to invisibilise public expressions of religiosity. Most participants reported that the ISIS (Islamic State of Iraq and the Levant) attacks had insidiously instilled anti-Muslim sentiment and honed a securitising approach towards Islam in the French political circles. While often depicting assimilation as undesirable and unattainable, our interlocutors perceived civic integration as a 'realistic' – but also necessary – aim for young people with an immigrant background.

The participants were broadly critical of mainstream politics. In addition to dissatisfaction with the functioning of current state of democracy and scepticism about the empowerment of citizens in the French institutional context, the young Muslim interlocutors were weary and frustrated with the current political order: most mentioned the rise of the radical populist right, anti-Muslim racism, and the rightward shift of Emmanuel Macron's The Republic on the Move – but they were even more critical of the media. They felt that the dominant media discourse was characterized by securitisation and nativist positions, and accused the French media of imposing an anti-Muslim agenda. Several interlocutors therefore prefer to follow current affairs on the social media. Consequently, the 'radicalisation' affecting a minority of Muslim youth seems to have been fuelled by two distinct factors: alienation from the majority values of French society on the one hand, and reaction against what they perceived as hostility to Islam and Muslims in public discourse on the other hand. As already discussed in Social Movements Theory, this is what Craig Calhoun (Citation2011) calls 'reactionary radicalism' and what Donatella Della Porta's (Citation2018) defines as relational radicalism, which can be translated as a process of 'going back to the basics' to express one's protest and discontent against the prevalent forms of essentialist and orientalist depiction of Islam in France. This article eventually challenged the conventional wisdom in European societies that presents Islam as a uniform religion. Instead, we tried to depict Islam as a phenomenon in minority contexts with diverse implications, practices, conventions, and traditions grounded in historical, social, and local settings.

*Acknowledgments: This article has benefitted considerably from a Horizon 2020 Prime Youth Project on youth co-radicalisation in Europe (Islam-ophob-ism, ERC AdG, Contract No. 785934, https://bpy.bilgi.edu.tr). We would like to thank Istanbul Bilgi University for the support received during the writing process of this article. We are grateful to the constructive criticisms made by the anonymous reviewers. Disclosure statement. No potential conflict of interest was reported by the authors. Additional information. Funding. The work was supported by the European Commission [ERC AdG 785934]. Journal of Contemporary European Studies (JCES) is a multidisciplinary journal for the empirical study of European societies, politics and cultures and is committed to the encouragement and promotion of debate on these topics. The central area focus of the journal is European in its broadest geographical definition and articles are welcomed from both cross-national and single-country specialists in European studies. The JCES differentiates itself from other European Studies journals in that it is not EU focused - its focus and interests extend beyond the EU - and in that it also provides a forum for debate about the theory and practice of 'area studies' and the advantages, scope and limitations of interdisciplinarity. Furthermore, the Journal is enhanced by non-European perspectives. Research and review articles are published in the JCES, as well as an extensive section containing reviews on recently published books relating to European areas and themes. The journal publishes articles from a variety of disciplines within the humanities and social sciences, including sociology and social policy, politics and economics. Recent issues have considered a range of themes including: gender, migration, labour, identity and integration. Thematic issues are regularly published and the Editorial*

*Board welcomes critical replies to articles that have appeared in earlier issues. Print ISSN: 1478-2804 Online ISSN: 1478-2790, 4 issues per year. Political drivers of Muslim youth radicalisation in France: religious radicalism as a response to nativism. Max-Valentin and Ayhan Kaya. Published online: 21 Mar 2023. To cite this article: Max-Valentin Robert & Ayhan Kaya (2023): Political drivers of Muslim youth radicalisation in France: religious radicalism as a response to nativism, Journal of Contemporary European Studies, Published online: 21 Mar 2023. Contact Ayhan Kaya ayhan.kaya@bilgi.edu.tr Department of International Relations, Istanbul Bilgi University, and Istanbul, Turkey. Journal of contemporary European Studies. © 2023 the Author(s). Published by Informa UK Limited, trading as Taylor & Francis Group.*

# Notes to Chapters

**Chapter 1: National Security Threat Perceptions and Countering Foreign Espionage Strategies: The EU and the French Security Reform**

1. The underlying causes of strategic surprise in EU foreign policy: a post-mortem investigation of the Arab uprisings and the Ukraine–Russia crisis of 2013/14.

2. Nikki Ikani and Christoph O.Meyer, European security-2022

3. The UK Big-3

4. The lessons of Eastern Europe for modern intelligence reform. Conflict, Security and Development, Volume 7, Number 4, December 2007

5. Pietro Castelli Gattinara and Caterina Froio: Politicizing Europe on the far right: Anti-EU mobilization across the party and non-party sector in France. Social Movement Studies-07 Jul 2021.

6. European Intelligence Oversight Network, the Stiftung Neue Verantwortung (SNV).

7. The UK Big-3: The French and German Intelligence Reforms, Intelligence Diversity and Foreign Espionage. Musa khan jalalzai.

4. Bruce Crumley. Were the Paris attacks a French intelligence failure? Al Jazeera November 17, 2015

5. 23 December 2022, BBC

6. Le Monde, 23 December 2022

7. 29 June 2022, the BBC Paris Correspondent Lucy Williamson report

8. Euro news on 09 July 2023-Le Monde, 28 October 2020

9. Alina Clasen. Intelligence reform and the transformation of the state: the end of a French exception German intelligence services point to increased hybrid security threats. EURACTIV.de-19 July 2023

10. Were the Paris attacks a French intelligence failure? Al Jazeera November 17, 2015

11. 23 December 2022, BBC

12. 28 October 2020, Paris based Le Monde Newspaper

13. 05 July 2016, Associated Press

14. 05 July 2016, New York Times (Aurelien Breeden).

15. Jacques Follorou. France's tepid intelligence reform, 07 June 2021, About Intel

16. Griff Witte and Loveday Morris. Failure to stop Paris attacks reveals fatal flaws at heart of European security-Washington Post, 28 November 2015

**Chaoter 2: The French Intelligence Reform, Jihadist Groups and the Threat of Radicalization, Nuclear and Biological Terrorism.**

1. John Wihbey and Leighton Walter Kille (France, Islam, terrorism and the challenges of integration: Research roundup, The Journalist's Resources. November 16, 2015.

2. 05 July 2016, New York Times

3. Ibid

4. Ibid

5. Anne Lise Michelot (Reform of the French Intelligence Oversight System, the Security Distillery- November 30, 2018.

6. Eric Denece. French Intelligence and Security Services in 2016, a Short History. Note, Historique No 47, December 2016. Centre Français de Recherche sur le Renseignement (CF2R).

7. Félix Tréguer (Intelligence Reform and the Snowden Paradox: The Case of France

8. Alex Mackenzie. Conspicuous by their absence? The member states in the European Union counter-terrorism. Journal of European Integration-11 September 2023.

9. Timothy Holman. 14 December 2015.

10. Ibid

11. Janani Krishnaswamy. Policy Report No-3, Why Intelligence Fails, the Hindu Centre for Politics and Public Policy-2013.

12. Timothy Holman. Paris: An Intelligence Failure or a Failure to Understand the Limits of Intelligence? Royal United Services Institute, London-14 December 2015

13. Janani Krishnaswamy. Policy Report No-3, Why Intelligence Fails, the Hindu Centre for Politics and Public Policy-2013.

14. Arab News. French spy row as Macron accuses intelligence chief of failure over Niger coup, 03 August 2023

15. On 27 April 2023, John Leicester (Intelligence chief: Russian spy ring had 'source' in France.

16. Ibid

131

17. Pakistan in the eye of thunderstorm. Musa Khan Jalalzai, 2022, India.
18. Ibid
19. The Taliban Misrule in Afghanistan. Musa Khan Jalalzai, 2022
20. Ibid
21. Ibid
22. The Stratfor report.
23. South Asia Democratic Forum. Policy Brief 10–Tablighi Jamaat and its role in Global Jihad. South Asia Democratic Forum-11 December 2020.
24. The DGSI report
25. Ibid
26. South Asia Democratic Forum. Policy Brief 10–Tablighi Jamaat and its role in Global Jihad. South Asia Democratic Forum 11 December 2020
27. Maria do Céu Pinto
28. Hindustan Times. Pakistan stood in support of Tablighi Jamaat, is Imran Khan going against Saudi Arabia? 24 December, 2021.

**Chapter 3: Intelligence Reform, Oversight Mechanism and the Role of CNCTR-National Commission, Foreign Espionage and Democratic Accountability.**

1. The Taliban Misrule in Afghanistan. Musa Khan Jalalzai, 2022
2. Le Monde April 27, 2023
4. Ibid
5. Gérard Davet and Fabrice Lhomme. The French secret service and its 'war chest' caught in the nets of the justice system, Le Monde, January 11, 2023
6. Davide Basso and Pekka Vanttinen in their analysis. France threatened by Russian spies 'under diplomatic cover'- EURACTIV, 28 April 2023
7. The UK Big-3. Musa Khan Jalalzai, 2022.
8. OpenDemocracy. France's surveillance: justice, freedom and security in the EU. Nicholas Hernanz, Julien Jeandesboz, Joanna Parkin, Francesco Ragazzi, Amandine Scherrer, Didier Bigo and Sergio Carrera- 14 May 2014'
9. Le Monde, 05 July 2023
10. John Keiger. The French riots threaten the state's very existence, Spectator Magazine, 02 July 2023.
11. Le Monde, 17 November 2018
12. Michael Jonsson. Expert Michael Jonsson-11 September 2023
13. John Psaropoulos. Europe awakens to the threat of sabotage by Russian agents, Al Ja zeera 17 Jan 2023

14. Intelligence reform and the transformation of the state: the end of a French exception. Olivier Chopin-22 May 2017

15. Damien Van Puyvelde. Intelligence, Democratic Accountability, and the Media in France-21 Aug 2014

16. Susana Sanz-Caballero. The concepts and laws applicable to hybrid threats, with a special focus on Europe. Humanities & Social Sciences Communications journal-29 June 2023

17. Bruce Crumley. Were the Paris attacks a French intelligence failure? Al Jazeera November 17, 2015)

18. Privacy International, December, 2021

19. Privacy international, 2018

20. Surveillance Technology Challenges Political Culture of Democratic States. Inez Miyamoto

21. Charles D. Ferguson in his paper. Assessing Radiological Weapons: Attack Methods and Estimated Effects. Defence against Terrorism Review Vol. 2, No. 2, fall 2009.

**Chapter 4: French Major intelligence and Law Enforcement reforms: Legal System and Intelligence Surveillance**

1. Christiaan Menkveld. Understanding the complexity of intelligence problems-08 Feb 2021

2. Felix Treguer in his paper. Major oversight gaps in the French intelligence legal framework. 25. March 2022

3. Felix Treguer. Major oversight gaps in the French intelligence legal framework. 25. March 2022

4. Journalist Jacques Follorou. Intelligence-gathering: French oversight board alarmed by the rise in requests concerning political activism. Le Monde 16 June, 2023

5. Associate researcher at CNRS and post-doctoral researcher at CERI Sciences Po in Paris, expert Félix Tréguer. Major oversight gaps in the French intelligence legal framework-25. March 2022

6. Ulrich Kelber. Aspects where Germany's draft Federal Intelligence Services Act misses the mark-16, February 2021

7. A Jean Monnet Professor ad personam in law at Queen Mary University of London and Emeritus Professor at Radboud University, Nijmegen, Netherlands, Elspeth Guild and head of Stiftung Neue Verantwortung's research on surveillance and democratic governance, and Intelligence expert, Thorsten Wetzlingin. Germany's BND Act & recent CJEU case law, 17. February 2021-About Intel.

8. Justine Victoria Valentin. The Polarization of the French society: a study of the Yellow Vests movement, SVF-3901. Faculty of Humanities, Social Science, and Education. Center for Peace Studies-May 2022.

9. Ibid

10. The UK Big-3: The French and German Intelligence Reforms, Intelligence Diversity and Foreign Espionage. Musa khan jalalzai.

11. The DW New report 15 May 2020

12. Electronic Frontier Foundation-14 January 2020

13. Danish Intelligence Oversight Board-May 2022

14. The Danish intelligence report (PET Report).

15. 12 January 2022, Charles Szumski. EURACTIV.com

16. Nikita Belukhin. The Scandal in Denmark's Military Intelligence: Too Much Transparency? Modern Diplomacy, 25 March 2022

17. The Danish Intelligence Oversight Board in its annual report

**Chapter 5: Overview of France's Intelligence Legal Framework. Félix Tréguer**

1. Tréguer, Félix. 2016. 'From Deep State Illegality to Law of the Land: The Case of Internet Surveillance in France'. https://halshs.archives-ouvertes.fr/halshs-01306332/ document (July 1, 2016).

2. See Loi n°2021-998 du 30 juillet 2021 relative à la prévention d'actes de terrorisme et au renseignement. Codified in the Code of Internal Security, Book VIII "On Intelligence" (article L. 801-L. 898-1).

3. Unless stated otherwise, all articles mentioned here are part of the Code of Internal Security.

4. Beyond the intelligence community, the décret n° 2015-1639 du 11 décembre 2015 relatif à la désignation des services autres que les services spécialisés de renseignement, autorisés à recourir aux techniques mentionnées au titre V du livre VIII du code de la sécurité intérieure opened the use of the surveillance techniques listed in the Intelligence Act to dozens of other agencies. The combined staff of these "second circle" agencies is over 45 000.

5. Interestingly, the 2014 DPR report advocated against the inclusion of MPs in the new oversight body, in light of the increased parliamentary control of intelligence services achieved in recent years through the DPR.

6. The non-binding nature of the CNCTR's ex ante oversight was criticised by the Bill's opponents. But as the 2014 DPR report had stressed a few weeks earlier, Urvoas and the government recalled that this was necessary to respect the Constitution's article 20 . According to the later, the government "shall have at its disposal the civil service and the armed forces." Since the CNCTR

is organically part of the executive branch, the Prime Minister –as head of the government– supposedly cannot be bound by its decisions.

7.  Report on the activity of the Parliamentary Delegation for Intelligence for the year 2019-2021 (June 2020), p. 61. Available at: https://data.guardint.org/en/entity/ 5fhfis4apmg?searchTerm=marge%20de%20progression&page=61

8.  See Loi n° 2007-1443 du 9 octobre 2007 . It was not until 2013, however, that the law was amended to substitute the word "contrôle" to that of "suivi," thereby recognising the delegation's oversight function.

9.  See Laurent, Sébastien Yves. 2015. 'Le Contrôle Parlementaire Du Renseignement (1971-2015): Les Enjeux Politiques d'une Tardive Banalisation'. In Mélanges En l'honneur de Bernard Lachaise, Riveneuve, 372–96..

10.  Full sentence in French: "il peut être imposé aux opérateurs et aux personnes mentionnés à l'article L. 851-1 la mise en oeuvre sur leurs réseaux de traitements automatisés destinés, en fonction de paramètres précisés dans l'autorisation, à détecter des connexions susceptibles de révéler une menace terroriste."

11.  Deep Packet Inspection a form of computer network packet filtering that examines the data part (content) –and possibly also the header (or metadata)– of a packet as it passes an inspection point (source: Wikipedia).

12.  See Délibération n° 2021-040 du 8 avril 2021 portant avis sur les articles 11 quinquies sexies et septies du projet de loi relatif a la prévention d'actes de terrorisme et au renseignement.

13.  Ibid. (§ 14 to 18).

14.  CJEU, La Quadrature du Net and Others v Premier Ministre and Others, §172-182.

15.  To comply with the CJEU however, the Council of State forced the government to "declare" such threats on national security every year with the adoption of an ad hoc executive decree.Conseil d'État, arrêt n°393099 du 21 avril 2021 (FDN et autres) (§44-46).

16.  Décision n° 2017-648 QPC du 4 août 2017 .

17.  The maximum duration for the retention of this data was originally one month. It was doubled by the reform of 2021, without the government providing information as to why such extension was necessary.

18.  T-CY Guidance Note #3 Transborder access to data (Article 32) (T-CY (2013)7 E). (2014). Council of Europe. https://www.coe.int/t/dghl/cooperation/ economiccrime/Source/Cybercrime/TCY /Guidance_Notes/T-CY%282013%297 REV_GN3_transborder_V11.pdf

19.  France Inter, "Gérald Darmanin : face au terrorisme, 'il ne faut être ni résigné ni outrancier'". Available at: https://www.franceinter.fr/emissions/l-invite-de-8h20-le-grandentretien/l-invite-de-8h20-le-grand-entretien-28-avril-2021

20. nGoodwin, B. (June 21, 2021). Secrecy around EncroChat cryptophone hack breaches French constitution, court hears. Computer-Weekly.com. Available at: https://www.computerweekly.com/news/252501921/ Secrecy-around-EncroChat- cryptophone-hack-breaches-French-constitution- court-hears.

21. See loi n°2018-607 du 13 juillet 2018, article 37.

22. On this legislative change, see also CNCTR's 2018 Annual Report, p. 28.

23. See the minutes of the Senate session where the amendment was introduced, May 22, 2018. www.senat.fr/seances/s201805/s20180522/s20180522022.html

24. Follorou, J. (2019, April 24). 'L'entrepôt, bâtiment ultrasécurisé et outil essential du renseignement français'. Le Monde. https://www.lemonde.fr/ societe/article/2019/04/24/l-entrepot-un-outil-essentiel-du-renseignement-qui-fonctionne-sans-cadre-legal_5454225_3224.html

25 'A French Alternative to Palantir Would Take Two Years to Make, Thales CEO Says'. December 8, 2020. Reuters. Available at: https://www.reuters.com/ article/ us-thales-ceo-idUSKBN2782FS.

26. Didier Bigo et al. National Security and Secret Evidence in Legislation and Before theCourts: Exploring the Challenges. Study for the European Parliament's Committee on Civil Liberties, Justice and Home Affairs PE 509.991. Brussels: European Parliament, 2014, p. 156.

27. Report on the activity of the Parliamentary Delegation for Intelligence for the year 2019-2020 (June 11, 2020).

28. 'FR-US Deal Unveiled', June 29, 2016. Intelligence Online. https: //www. intelligenceonline.com/government-intelligence_organizations/2016/06/29/ spins--fr-us-deal-unveiled,108172546-art

29. See CNCTR Annual Report 2018, p. 50.

30. ECHR, Big Brother Watch and others v. United Kingdom (Grand Chamber Judgment), May, 25 2021, § 362)

31. Surveillance by intelligence services: fundamental rights safeguards and remedies in the EU Volume II: field perspectives and legal update, Fundamental Rights Agency (2017), p. 52. Available at: https://data.guardint. org/en/entity/0t6462gq7i1d?page=52

32. See CNCTR Annual Report 2017, p. 85-86.

33. Report on the activity of the Parliamentary Delegation for Intelligence for the year 2019-2020 (June 11, 2020). Available at:https://data.guardint.org/en/ entity/5fhfis4apmg?page=100

34. Quoted in Valdiguié, L. November, 16 2020. 'Le programme "X", un logiciel espion surpuissant pour traquer les terroristes'. https://www.marianne.net/ societe/terrorisme/ le-programme-x-un-logiciel-espion-surpuissant-pour-traquer-les-terroristes.

35. Ibid.

36. Report on the activity of the Parliamentary Delegation for Intelligence for the year 2019-2020 (June 11, 2020). Available at: https://data.guardint.org/en/entity/5fhfis4apmg?page=266

37. Ibid

38. Anderson, D. Report of the Bulk Powers Review. Independent Reviewer of Terrorism Legislation (August 2016).

39. The range of abuses that can be reported are limited to criminal violations of the confidentiality of communications. Cases of active corruption, for instance, are not covered. What is more, a last-minute governmental amendment deleted the sentence granting po-tential whistleblowers the right to "testify about classified information, information that might harm the security of personnels, or undermine the missions of intelligence agencies." This creates huge legal insecurity for potential whistleblowers.

40. The Global Principles on National Security and the Right to Information (Tshwane Principles). 2013. Open Justice Initiative. Available at: https://www.opensocietyfoundations.org/publications/global-principles-national-security-and-freedom-information-tshwane-principles.

## Chapter 6: Intelligence Reform and the Snowden Paradox: The Case of France. Félix Tréguer

Association des Services Internet Communautaires. (2013, March 18). Surveillance de l'Internet, accès aux données d'utilisateurs: Pour un moratoire sur les régimes d'exception. Association des Sites Internet Communautaires. Retrieved from http://archive.is/firXs

Benkler, Y. (2011). A free irresponsible press: Wikileaks and the battle over the soul of the networked fourth estate. Harvard Civil Rights-Civil Liberties Law Review, 46(2), 311–397.

Bigo, D., Carrera, S., Hernanz, N., & Scherrer, A. (2014). National security and secret evidence in legislation and before the courts: Exploring the challenges (Report to the European Parliament's Committee on Civil Liberties, Justice and Home Affairs [LIBE] No. PE 509.991). Brussels: European Parliament. Retrieved from http://www.europarl.europa.eu/thinktank/fr/ document. html?reference=IPOL_STU% 282014%295 09991

Breindl, Y. (2011). Hacking the law: An analysis of internet-based campaigning on digital rights in the European Union. Brussels: Free University of Brussels.

Buzan, B., & Wæver, O. (2003). Regions and powers: The structure of international security. Cambridge: Cambridge University Press.

Campbell, D. (2000). Inside Echelon: The history, structure, and function of the global surveillance system known as Echelon. Telepolis. Retrieved from https://www.heise.de/tp/features/Inside-Echelon-3447440. html

Chapuis, N. (2013, June 12). Urvoas: "Je n'ai pas rencontré de programme de surveillance similaire en France". Le Monde. Retrieved from http://www. lemonde.fr/politique/article/2013/06/12/urvoas-jen-ai-pas-rencontre-de-programme-de-surveillancesimilaire-en-france_3428507_823448.html

Chevallier, J. (1992). Le mythe de la transparence administrative. In Information et transparence administrative (pp. 239–275). Paris: Presses Universitaires de France.

Cybercrime Convention Committee. (2014). T-CY Guidance Note #3 transborder access to data (No. T-CY [2013]7 E). Strasbourg: Council of Europe. Retrieved from https://www.coe.int/t/dghl/cooperation/economiccrime/ Source/Cybercrime/TCY/Guidance_Notes/T-CY%282013%297REV_ GN3_transborder_V11.pdf

EFF. (2014). Necessary & proportionate: International principles on the application of Human Rights to communications surveillance. Retrieved from https://en.necessaryandproportionate.org

Errera, R. (2003). Les origines de la loi française du 10 juillet 1991 sur les écoutes téléphoniques. Revue Trimestrielle des Droits de l'Homme, 55, 851–870.

Fédération Internationale des Droits de l'Homme. (2013, July 12). Affaire Snowden: La FIDH saisit l'ONU. FIDH. Retrieved from https://archive.is/mSEZo

Follorou, J. (2013, October 30). Surveillance: La DGSE a transmis des données à la NSA américaine. Le Monde. Retrieved from http://www.lemonde.fr/internation al/article/2013/10/30/surveillance-la-dgse-a-transm is-des-donnees-a-la-nsa-americaine 3505266 3210. html

Follorou, J., & Johannès, F. (2013, July 4). La totalité de nos communications espionnées par un supercalculateur. Le Monde. Retrieved from http://www. lemonde.fr/ societe/article/2013/07/04/revelations -sur-le-big-brother-francais_3441973_3224.html

French Government. (2008). Livre blanc sur la défense et la sécurité nationale. Paris: French Government.

French Government. (2015, November 19). #Antiterrorisme: Manuel Valls annonce des mesures exceptionnelles. Paris: French Government. Retrieved from http://archive.is/x1zhB

French National Assembly. (2013). Audition du préfet Erard Corbin de Mangoux, Directeur Général de la sécurité extérieure (DGSE) au ministère de la Défense (Compte Rendu n° 56). Paris: French National Assembly.

French Presidency. (2014, July 9). Compte-rendu public du Conseil national du renseignement. Retrieved from https://archive.is/7W2jm

Fuster, G. G. (2014). The emergence of personal data protection as a fundamental right of the EU. Berlin: Springer Science+Business.

Giroux, H. A. (2014). ISIS and the spectacle of terrorism: Resisting mainstream workstations of fear. Philosophers for Change. Retrieved from https://philosoph ersforchange.org/2014/10/07/isis-and-the-spectacle -of-terrorism-resisting-mainstream-workstations-offear

Hintz, A., & Dencik, L. (2016). The politics of surveillance policy: UK regulatory dynamics after Snowden. Internet Policy Review, 5(3). doi:10.14763/2016.3.424

Hourdeaux, J. (2016, June 6). Comment les services de renseignement ont mis en place une surveillance

générale du Net dès 2009. Mediapart. Retrieved from https://www.mediapart.fr/journal/france/0606 16/comment-les-services-de-renseignement-ont-mis -en-place-une-surveillance-generale-du-net-des-2009

Jauvert, V. (2015, July 1). Comment la France écoute (aussi) le monde. Le Nouvel Observateur. Retrieved from http://tempsreel.nouvelobs.com/societe/2015 0625.OBS1569/exclusif-comment-la-france-ecouteaussi-le-monde.html

Joinet, L. (2013). Mes raisons d'État: Mémoires d'un épris de justice. Bayonne: La Découverte.

La Quadrature du Net. (2013, July 29). Newsletter #51. LQDN. Retrieved from https://www.laquadrature. net/fr/newsletter/newsletter-51

Lyon, D. (2015). Surveillance after Snowden. Cambridge: Polity Press.

Mailland, J. (2001). Freedom of speech, the internet, and the costs of control: The French example. New York University Journal of International Law & Politics, 33.

Manach, J. M. (2010, October 2). Frenchelon: La DGSE est en "1ère division". Le Monde. Retrieved from http://bugbrother.blog.lemonde.fr/2010/10/02/fren chelon-la-dgse-est-en-1ere-division

Manach, J.-M. (2013, July 11). La DGSE a le "droit" d'espionner ton Wi-Fi, ton GSM et ton GPS aussi. Le Monde. Retrieved from http://bugbrother.blog. lemonde.fr/2013/07/11/la-dgse-a-le-droit-despionn er-ton-wi-fi-ton-gsm-et-ton-gps-aussi

Marzouki, M. (2009). "Non à Edvige": Sursaut ou prise de conscience? Plein Droit, 80, 21–26. Retrieved from http://www.gisti.org/spip.php?article1477

Meili, S. (1998). Cause lawyers and social movements: A comparative perspective on democratic change in Argentina and Brazil. In A. Sarat & S. Scheingold (Eds.), Cause lawyering: Political commitments and professional responsibilities (pp. 487–522). Oxford: Oxford University Press.

Meyer, T., & Audenhove, L. V. (2012). Surveillance and regulating code: An analysis of graduated response in France. Surveillance & Society, 9(4), 365–377.

Reflects.info. (2016, June 6). Qosmos et le gouvernement Français, très à l'écoute du Net dès 2009. Reflects.info. Retrieved from https://reflets.info/qosmos-et-le-gouvernement-francais-tres-a-lecoutedu-net-des-2009

Rubinstein, I. S., Nojeim, G. T., & Lee, R. D. (2014). Systematic government access to personal data: A comparative analysis. International Data Privacy Law, 4(2), 96–119.

Schulhofer, S. (2015). Access to national security information under the U.S. Freedom of Information Act (Public Law Research Paper No. 15–14). New York, NY:NYU School of Law. Retrieved from https://papers. ssrn.com/abstract=2610901

Schulze, M. (2015). Patterns of surveillance legitimization. The German discourse on the NSA scandal. Surveillance & Society, 13(2), 197–217.

Tarrow, S. (2015). War, states, and contention: A comparative historical study (1st ed.). Ithaca and London: Cornell University Press.

Tarrow, S. (2016). Close interaction, incompatible regimes, contentious challenges: The transnational movement to protect privacy. Berlin: Berlin Social Science Center. Retrieved from https://www.research gate.net/project/Transnational-Movements-and-the -Protection-of-Privacy/update/582c8dc608ae91d0fe 24f203

Tilly, C., & Tarrow, S. (2015). Contentious politics (2nd ed.). New York, NY: Oxford University Press.

Tréguer, F. (2015). Hackers vs states: Subversion, repression and resistance in the online public sphere. Droit et Société, 91(3), 639–652.

Tréguer, F. (2016a). From deep state illegality to law of the land: The case of internet surveillance in France. Paper presented at the 7th Biennial Surveillance & Society Conference (SSN 2016) "Power, Performance and Trust", Barcelona, Spain. Retrieved from https://halshs.archives-ouvertes.fr/halshs-01306332 / document

Tréguer, F. (2016b). French constitutional council strikes down 'Blank Check' provision in the 2015 Intelligence Act. Retrieved from https://halshs.archive-souvertes.fr/halshs-01399550/document UK Home Office. (2016). Operational case for bulk powers. London: British Government. Retrieved from https://www.gov.uk/government/uploads/system/up     loads/attachment_data/file/504187/Operational_Ca se_for_Bulk_Powers.pdf

Urvoas, J.-J. (2013a, July 4). Big Brother à la française? Commentaires. Retrieved from http://archive.is/7SGgk

Urvoas, J.-J. (2013a, October 30). Il faut renforcer le contrôle des services de renseignement en France. Le Monde. Retrieved from http://www.lemonde.fr/idees/article/2013/10/30/il-faut-renforcer-le-contro le-des-services-de-renseignement-en-france_35051 16_3232.html

Urvoas, J.-J., & Verchère, P. (2013). Rapport en conclusion des travaux d'une mission d'information sur l'évaluation du cadre juridique applicable aux services de renseignement (Commission des Lois No. 1022). Paris: National Assembly. Retrieved from http://www.assemblee-nationale.fr/14/controle/lois / renseignement.asp

Wetzling, T. (2016). The key to intelligence reform in Germany (Europäische Digitale Agenda). Retrieved from http://www.stiftung-nv.de/sites/default/files/ snv_g10.pdf

Woods, L. (2016, December 21). Data retention and national law: The ECJ ruling in Joined Cases C-203/15 and C-698/15 Tele2 and Watson (Grand Chamber). EU Law Analysis. Retrieved from https://eulaw analysis.blogspot. fr/2016/12/data-retention-and-national-law-ecj.html

**Chapter 7: Espionage by Europeans: Treason and Counterintelligence in Post-Cold war Europe. Michael Jonsson**

1. Mearsheimer, "Bound to Fail." 24.

2. Cunliffe, "Hard target espionage."

3. Cunliffe, "Hard target espionage," 1018.

4. Olson, To Catch a Spy, 25.

5. Jones and Rathbone, "Tip of the iceberg,"

6. Rathbone, "On a par with the Russians."

7. Raik, "Liberalism and geopolitics in EU – Russia relations."

8. Brandt and Taussig, "Europe's Authoritarian Challenge."; Bowen, 'Russian military intelligence."

9. Ilves and Giles, "Why can't Europe see that it's at war with Russia?"

10. Cited in France 24, "Europe on alert as Russia steps up aggressive spying."

11. Swedish Security Service, Säkerhetspolisen 2021, 13–16; Kaitsepolitseiamet, Estonian Internal Security Service 2021–2022, 2, 21; Finnish Security and Intelligence Service, "Foreign Intelligence and Influence Operations"; Bundesamt **für** Verfassungsschutz, Brief summary 2021 Report, 44–48.

12. Data for this article was originally compiled in Jonsson and Gustafsson, Espionage by Europeans 2010–2021.

The article however elaborates certain strands of the analysis to address specific debates in the intelligence studies literature, and updates and complements data where possible, while excluding other topics.

13. C.f. Fischer "My two moles"; Thompson, "Toward an updated understanding of espionage motivation"; Hatfield, "An ethical defense of treason"; and Kerr, "Investigating Soviet espionage and subversion."

14. Taylor and Snow, "Cold war spies", 101. For an example of a non-Anglo-Saxon case that has received outsize attention see Swedish colonel Stig Wennerström, Agrell Stig Wennerström, Widen 'The Wennerström spy case'.

15. Taylor and Snow, Cold war spies, 101.

16. Taylor and Snow, Cold war spies, 115–116.

17. Taylor and Snow, Cold war spies, 109, 115.

18. A parallel can be drawn to research on terrorism, which was previously criticised for i.a. being overly reliant on single-case studies, or first-hand accounts of former intelligence practitioners. Silke, 'The Devil You Know'.

19. Herbig, The Expanding Spectrum of Espionage by Americans; Herbig, Changes in Espionage by Americans: 1947–2007.; Herbig and Wiskoff Espionage Against the United States by American Citizens 1947–2001; Wood and Wiskoff Americans Who Spied Against Their Country Since World War II.

20. Herbig, The Expanding Spectrum, v-vi.

21. As opposed to terrorism-related cases, where Europol annually publishes a study on recent European cases. C.f. Europol, European Union Threat and Situation Report 2022.

22. Jurvee and Perling, Russia's espionage in Estonia, 3.

23. Lillbacka, "The social context as a predictor," 118, 134, 135–138.

24. Macrakis, "Does effective espionage lead to success in science and technology?"

25. This refers to CiCentre.com, an online resource that has a set of 'international' (i.e., non-American) cases.

26. Beyond the European Union members, the study also includes Norway, the UK, Albania and Monte Negro.

27. This definition follows i.a. Hatfield, "the betrayal of secret information rather than covert paramilitary action", in Hatfield, "An ethical defense of treason" 195.

28. Bergqvist"Nätverket som kartlade försvarets hemligheter".

29. For reasons of brevity, cases that were excluded from the sample are not listed in full. The criteria have however been strictly interpreted, and exclusion of relevant cases is more likely than inclusion of irrelevant ones.

30. While the aim is to make the article comparable to Herbig et al, there are many similarities to the challenges described by for instance Taylor and Snow, Cold war spies, 101–102.

31. European countries have varied greatly on what policy they have adopted. Ferris-Rotman and Nakashima, 'Estonia knows a lot about battling Russian spies'.

32. That is, the dominance of Russia as an instigator (37 of 42 cases), the prevalence of male spies (40 of 42), or the clustering of cases in the Baltic countries (30 of 42) would not shift decisively by adding individual cases.

33. This includes four Russian illegals – for whom recruitment, motives for espionage and so forth are moot points – and three cases of individuals who were publicly accused of espionage, but so far not prosecuted.

34. Deutsche Welle, "Estonian couple arrested for giving secrets to Russia"; Äripäev, "Dressen luuras".

35. Deutsche Welle, "German-Afghan spy".

36. Viktoria received six years' incarceration with five years' probation, compared to Aleksei's 16 years (ERR 'Dressen Convicted of Treason'.) The wife of a German-Afghan translator received a ten-month suspended sentence, while he was sentenced to six years and ten months (Deutsche Welle, 'German-Afghan spy'.).

37. Pannett, "Germany says wife of man believed to be double agent".

38. Kramer, "A Weak Link in NATO?"

39. As noted previously, four cases of illegals are excluded from the main sample (category A+B), but included in a miscellaneous category (D), which is however not included in the graphs and tables.

40. See the case of Gwendolyn and Walter Kendall Myers, who spied for Cuban intelligence for almost three decades. As in the European cases, Gwendolyn acted as an accomplice to Kendall, and received a much more lenient sentence than her husband. Cf Herbig, The Expanding Spectrum of Espionage, 20–21. For a more recent case, see Jonathan and Diana Toebbe. Associated Press 'A Navy nuclear engineer and his wife'.

41. For instance Marta Rita Velazquez, who recruited the better-known Ana Belen Montes to spy at the U.S. DIA on behalf of the the Cuban Intelligence Directorate. Herbig, The Expanding Spectrum of Espionage, 11–12.

42. Herbig, The Expanding Spectrum of Espionage, 9–11.

43. Herbig, The Expanding Spectrum of Espionage, 11.

44. Herbig, The Expanding Spectrum of Espionage, 9, 12.

45. For the 39 individuals for whom the age at the time espionage began was possible to determine, the median age was in the late 30s, notably late in life for first-time offenders in most categories of high-risk criminality.

46. C.f. Herbig, The Expanding Spectrum of Espionage, 12.

47. The Baltic Times, "Dressen profile perfect fit for FSB"; BNS, "Estonian court jails former ISS employee".

48. Whereas the exact date of recruitment is hard to tell, two were below 20, three between 20–29 and one 30–39. Laine, "FSB hired local thug"; Koorits, "Kapo aastaraamat"; Roonemaa, "How smuggler helped Russia".

49. Weiss, "The hero who betrayed".

50. For a methodological discussion, see Jonsson, A Farewell to Arms, 61–78.

51. Weiss, "The hero who betrayed".

52. Roonemaa, "How smuggler helped Russia".

53. Amongst the 11 individuals who reported to have been coerced into espionage, 6 had double citizenship (Russian and Estonian), one was an Estonian with Russian parents, one a Russian student in Estonia, one a Latvian farmer with a business in Russia, one a Lithuanian politician – and one recruited by the Belarusian KGB.

54. Beyond 6 Russian-Estonian smugglers, and the Estonian officer, also see Roonemaa 'Spiegs, ko Krievija aizmirsa'; Springe, 'Uzdevums noskaidrot vai latvija'.

55. Toda, "The sweet life of Russian spies".

56. Schindler, "NATO's big new Russian spy scandal".

57. Herbig, The Expanding Spectrum of Espionage, 44–49. Money was a prevalent motive in earlier cohorts too

58. This refers to surface-level factors, often weeded out during the process of getting a security clearance. For an insightful discussion of motivational factors that are harder to observe, or how life-events may affect would-be spies, see Thompson, 'Toward an updated understanding of espionage motivation'.

59. This refers to Alexei Dressen, an employee of the Estonian Internal Security Service (ISS) who spied for the Russian FSB. See Anvelt, 'Raivo Aeg: riigireetur tegutses aastaid'.. An Austrian officer spying for the GRU reportedly had 'drunken sojourns' in luxury hotels abroad. See Toda, 'The sweet life of Russian spies'.

60. In 1990–2015, 98 per cent of American spies were likewise heterosexual. Herbig, The Expanding Spectrum, 10.

61. Weiss, "The hero who betrayed".

62. Schindler, "NATO's big new Russian spy scandal".

63. For a similar argument, c.f. Burkett, "An Alternative Framework for Agent Recruitment".

64. Hence, moles eloped detection for longer, remaining active on average 7.4 years vs 4.4 years for others.

65. Herbig, The Expanding Spectrum, 8. The percentage of male perpetrators has varied between 88 and 95 per cent. In 1990–2015, the median age when

Americans began spying was just north of 40, whereas in 1980–89, it was slightly below 30, and in 1947–79, the median spy was in his early 30s when the treason began.

66. Ibid, 15. The share of uniformed military amongst convicted spies has shrunk to approximately one quarter in the U.S. in 1990–2015, compared to half during both 1947–1979, and 1980–1989.

67. C.f. Roonemaa, "How smuggler helped Russia".

68. Herbig, The Expanding Spectrum, 36; C.f. The Guardian, 'FBI and MI5 leaders give unprecedented'.

69. In total, 37 individuals were convicted for spying on behalf of Russia. For 5 of these, it was however not possible to ascertain which Russian service had recruited the spy.

70. The Guardian, "FBI and MI5 leaders give unprecedented".

71. For an in-depth analysis of contemporary Chinese espionage, see Joske, Spies and Lies.

72. See Reuters, "Retired German political scientist". and Der Spiegel, "Früherer BND-Informant". Also c.f. Moens, "Belgium probes top EU think-tanker".

73. Reuters, "China reported to have tried to recruit".

74. Barry and Kolata, "China's Lavish Funds Lured U.S. Scientists".

75. See i.a. Plucinska, Qing, Ptak and Stecklow, "Special report: How Poland became a front".

76. Two individuals that were listed as suspected have since been convicted in Germany (see Der Spiegel 'Früherer BND-Informant'); and a woman has been convicted in Estonia for acting as an accomplice to an already convicted spy (ERR, 'Court jails Estonian'.). Three French nationals – two of whom were erstwhile DGSE officers – were also incarcerated in 2020 for spying on behalf of China (see Rogan 'France spy scandal'.).

77. SVT Nyheter, "Bröder döms för grovt spioneri".

78. Granlund, "Gift par från Ryssland gripna för spionage".

79. Janicek, "Slovaks charge 2 with spying for Russia's military service".

80. Deutsche Welle, "German soldier accused of espionage".

81. Hill, "German intelligence officer arrested".

82. Including four Russian nationals, who were all convicted for espionage in Estonia.

83. Bayer, "Brussels, city of spies"; Moens, "Belgium's spy problem"; Deutsche Welle, "Hundreds of Russian and Chinese spies in Brussels".

84. Ferris-Rotman and Nakashima, "Estonia knows a lot".

85. See for instance Shlapak and Johnson, Deterrence on NATO's Eastern Flank.

86. Weiss, "The hero who betrayed"; Ferris-Rotman and Nakashima, "Estonia knows a lot".

87. Lucas, "Estonian espionage is far from an embarrassment".

88. Moens, "The EU has a spy problem".

89. Researcher Kenneth Lasoen, as quoted in Moens, "The EU has a spy problem".

90. Ints Ulmanis, as quoted in Springe, "How Latvia is (not) catching Russian spies".

91. Willoughby, "Uncertainty over whether Czech accused of spying for Russians".

92. Jurvee and Perling, Russia's espionage in Estonia, 1–2.

93. Hedenskog and Persson 'Russian Security Policy', Oxenstierna and Westerlund (eds) Russian Military Capability in a Ten-Year Perspective 2019, 83–85.

94. C.f., Ferris-Rotman and Nakashima 'Estonia knows a lot'.

95. European countries that consider Russia as their 'dominant threat by far' (the Baltic countries, Poland and Finland) also saw the vast majority of convictions. By contrast, in the 14 European countries that took a dimmer view of the Russian threat ('not a threat'/'there are other, more significant threats') only 2 spies were convicted in total in 11 years. C.f. Meijer and Brooks, "Illusions of Autonomy", 17.

96. A preliminary overview of recent cases – not included in Appendix A – suggests that between December 2021 and January 2023, there have been at least seven convictions for espionage on behalf of Russia and three on behalf of China, with only one of these individuals under investigation (category C) in the Appendix.

97. There are a number of espionage cases in European non-NATO/EU member countries, particularly those with a fraught relation to Russia. See for instance Lapaiev, "The political dimensions of Russia's spy games in Ukraine"; Feifer, "Georgia says 13 alleged Russian spies arrested"; Guardian, (Citation2010) "Georgia arrests six more suspected Russian spies"; Radio Free Europe/Radio Liberty (Citation2018) "Former Moldovan lawmaker sentenced to 14 years"; Karaman "Turkish intelligence cracks down on Russian spy network".

98. Weiss "The hero who betrayed".

99. Toda, "A Russian spy's manual".

100.    Schindler, "NATO's big new Russian spy scandal".

101.    Baltic Times "Dressen profile perfect fit for FSB".

102.    SVT Nyheter "FOI-forskaren om spionbröderna".

103.    C.f. Silke "The Devil You Know", and how terrorism studies has since evolved into a more mature field of research, benefiting from a broader range of methodological approaches complementing each other.

## Bibliography

Agrell, W. Stig Wennerström: Myten om en svensk storspion. Stockholm: Appell Förlag, 2020. [Google Scholar]

Anvelt, K. "Raivo Aeg: riigireetur tegutses aastaid." Eesti Ekspress, February 23, 2012. [Google Scholar]

Äripäev "Dressen luuras Vene heaks aastaid." April 12, 2013. [Google Scholar]

Associated Press. "A Navy Nuclear Engineer and His Wife Enter New Guilty Pleas in Submarine-Secrets Case." NPR, September 27, 2022. [Google Scholar]

Baltic Times, The "Dressen Profile Perfect Fit for FSB." July 25, 2012. [Google Scholar]

Barry, E., and G. Kolata "China's Lavish Funds Lured U.S. Scientists. What Did It Get in Return?" The New York Times, February 6, 2020. [Google Scholar]

Bayer, L. "Brussels, City of Spies", Politico, August 21, 2018. [Google Scholar]

Bergqvist, U. "Nätverket som kartlade försvarets hemligheter." Sveriges Radio, October 6, 2021. [Google Scholar]

BNS. "Estonian Court Jails Former ISS Employee for Spying for Russia." October 4, 2019. [Google Scholar]

Brandt, J., and T. Taussig. "Europe's Authoritarian Challenge." The Washington Quarterly 42, no. 4 (2019): 133–153. doi:10.1080/0163660X.2019.1693099. [Taylor & Francis Online] [Web of Science ®], [Google Scholar]

Bundesamt für Verfassungsschutz. Brief summary 2021 Report of the Protection of the Constitution. Facts and Trends. Berlin, June 7, 2022. [Google Scholar]

Burkett, R. "An Alternative Framework for Agent Recruitment: From MICE to RASCLS." Studies in Intelligence 57, no. 1 (2013): 7–17. [Google Scholar]

Cunliffe, K. S. "Hard Target Espionage in the Information Era: New Challenges for the Second Oldest Profession." Intelligence & National Security 36, no. 7 (2021): 1018–1034. doi:10.1080/02684527.2021.1947555. [Taylor & Francis Online] [Web of Science ®], [Google Scholar]

Der Spiegel. "Früherer BND-Informant und Ehefrau wegen Spionage verurteilt." April 29, 2022. [Google Scholar]

Deutsche Welle. "Estonian Couple Arrested for Giving Secrets to Russia." February 22, 2012. [Google Scholar]

Deutsche Welle. "German-Afghan Spy Gets Nearly 7 Years for Treason." March 24, 2020. [Google Scholar]

Deutsche Welle. "German Soldier Accused of Espionage Faces Trial." November 8, 2022. [Google Scholar]

Deutsche Welle. "Hundreds of Russian and Chinese Spies in Brussels – Report." February 9, 2019. [Google Scholar]

ERR. "Court Jails Estonian Woman Found Guilty of Spying for China" June 4, 2022. [Google Scholar]

ERR. "Dressen Convicted of Treason, Gets 16 Years." July 3, 2012. [Google Scholar]

Europol European Union Threat and Situation Report 2022 (TE-SAT), The Hague, July 2022. [Google Scholar]

Feifer, G. "Georgia Says 13 Alleged Russian Spies Arrested." Radio Free Europe/ Radio Liberty, November 5, 2010. [Google Scholar]

Ferris-Rotman, A., and E. Nakashima "Estonia Knows a Lot About Battling Russian Spies, and the West is Paying Attention." Washington Post, March 27, 2018. [Google Scholar]

Finnish Security and Intelligence Service. "Foreign Intelligence and Influence Operations." Accessed November 25, 2022. https://supo.fi/en/intelligence-and-influence-operations. [Google Scholar]

Fischer, B. B. "My Two Moles: A Memoir." International Journal of Intelligence & CounterIntelligence 31, no.1 [ 2021] 2022: 147–163. doi:10.1080/08850607.2 021.1888041. [Taylor & Francis Online], [Google Scholar]

France 24. "Europe on Alert as Russia Steps Up Aggressive Spying", April 16, 2021. [Google Scholar]

Granlund, J. "Gift par från Ryssland gripna för spionage – levde stillsamt villaliv" Aftonbladet, November 22, 2022. [Google Scholar]

Guardian, the "Georgia Arrests Six More Suspected Russian Spies", December 7, 2010. [Google Scholar]

Guardian, T "FBI and MI5 Leaders Give Unprecedented Joint Warning on Chinese Spying." July 7, 2022. [Google Scholar]

Hatfield, J. M. "An Ethical Defense of Treason by Means of Espionage." Intelligence & National Security 32, no. 2 (2017): 195–207. doi:10.1080/02684527.2016 .1248571. [Taylor & Francis Online] [Web of Science ⁎], [Google Scholar]

Hedenskog, J., and G. Persson, "Russian Security Policy." In Russian Military Capability in a Ten-Year Perspective 2019, edited by S. Oxenstierna and F. Westerlund, 79–96. Stockholm: Swedish Defence Research Agency, 2019 December [Google Scholar]

Herbig, K. L. Changes in Espionage by Americans: 1947–2007, Technical Report 08-05. Monterey CA: U.S. Dept. of Defence, March 2008. [Crossref], [Google Scholar]

Herbig, K. L. The Expanding Spectrum of Espionage by Americans, 1947–2015, Technical Report 17-10. Monterey CA: U.S. Dept. of Defence, August 2017. [Google Scholar]

Herbig, K. L., and M. F. Wiskoff Espionage Against the United States by American Citizens 1947–2001, Technical Report 02-5. Monterey CA: U.S. Dept. of Defence, July 2002. [Google Scholar]

Hill, T. "German Intelligence Officer Arrested on Suspicion of Spying for Russia" Associated Press, December 23, 2022. [Google Scholar]

Ilves, T. H., and K. Giles (2021) "Why Can't Europe See That It's at War with Russia?" The Telegraph, April 23, 2021. [Google Scholar]

Janicek, K. "Slovaks Charge 2 with Spying for Russia's Military Service" Associated Press, March 15, 2022. [Google Scholar]

Jones, S., and J. P. Rathbone "'Tip of the iceberg': Rise of Russian Spying Activity Alarms European Capitals." Financial Times, March 27, 2022. [Google Scholar]

Jonsson, M. A Farewell to Arms. Motivational Change and Diverge Inside FARC-EP 2002-2010. Uppsala: Acta Universitatis Upsaliensis, 2014. [Google Scholar]

Jonsson, M., and J. Gustafsson. Espionage by Europeans 2010-2021. A Preliminary Review of Court Cases. Stockholm: FOI, 2022. [Google Scholar]

Joske, A. Spies and Lies: How China's Greatest Covert Operations Fooled the World. Melbourne: Hardie Grant Books, 2022. [Google Scholar]

Jurvee, I., and L. Perling. Russia's Espionage in Estonia: A Quantitative Analysis of Convictions. Tallinn: International Centre for Defence and Security, 2019. November. [Google Scholar]

Kaitsepolitseiamet. Estonian Internal Security Service 2021-2022. Tallinn: Kapo, 2022 April. [Google Scholar]

Karaman, N. "Turkish Intelligence Cracks Down on Russian Spy Network" Daily Sabah, June 1, 2022. [Google Scholar]

Kerr, S. "Investigating Soviet Espionage and Subversion: The Case of Donald Maclean." Intelligence & National Security 17, no. 1 (2002): 101–116. doi:10.1080/02684520412331306430. [Taylor & Francis Online], [Google Scholar]

Koorits, V. "Kapo aastaraamat: kapo tabas eelmisel aastal viis Venemaa kasuks luuranud meest, neist kolm juhtumit olid seni teadmata." Delfi April 12, 2018. [Google Scholar]

Kramer, M. A Weak Link in NATO? Bulgaria, Russia and the Lure of Espionage. Cambridge, Massachusetts: Davis Center for Russian and Eurasian Studies, Harvard University, April 1, 2021. [Google Scholar]

Kristie Macrakis, K. "Does Effective Espionage Lead to Success in Science and Technology? Lessons from the East German Ministry for State Security." Intelligence & National Security 19, no. 1 (2004): 52–77. doi:10.1080/0268452 042000222920. [Taylor & Francis Online], [Google Scholar]

Laine, M. "FSB Hired Local Thug to Keep an Eye on Border Guard." Postimees April 15, 2019. [Google Scholar]

Lapaiev, Y. "The Political Dimensions of Russia's Spy Games in Ukraine." Eurasia Daily Monitor 17: 60 April 30, 2020. [Google Scholar]

Lillbacka, R. "The Social Context as a Predictor of Ideological Motives for Espionage." International Journal of Intelligence & CounterIntelligence 30, no. 1 (2017): 117–146. doi:10.1080/08850607.2016.1230704. [Taylor & Francis Online] [Web of Science *], [Google Scholar]

Lucas, E. "Estonian Espionage is Far from an Embarrassment." Politico, February 29, 2012. [Google Scholar]

Mearsheimer, J. J. "Bound to Fail: The Rise and Fall of the Liberal World Order." International Security 43, no. 4 (2019) (Spring 2019): 7–50. doi:10.1162/ ISEC_a_00342. [Crossref] [Web of Science *], [Google Scholar]

Meijer, H., and S. G. Brooks. "Illusions of Autonomy: Why Europe Cannot Provide for Its Security if the United States Pulls Back." International Security 45, no. 4 (2021): 7–43. doi:10.1162/isec_a_00405. [Crossref] [Web of Science *], [Google Scholar]

Moens, B. "Belgium Probes Top EU Think-Tanker for Links to China." Politico, September 18, 2020a. [Google Scholar]

Moens, B. "Belgium's Spy Problem." Politico, September 29, 2020b. [Google Scholar]

Moens, B. "The EU Has a Spy Problem – Here's Why It's so Difficult to Catch Them." Politico, December 1, 2022. [Google Scholar]

Olson, J. M. To Catch a Spy: The Art of Counterintelligence. Washington DC: Georgetown University Press, 2021. [Google Scholar]

Pannett, R. "Germany Says Wife of Man Believed to Be Double Agent Also Helped Spy for China." Washington Post, August 3, 2021. [Google Scholar]

Plucinska, J., K. G. Qing, A. Ptak, and S. Stecklow "Special Report: How Poland Became a Front in the New Cold War Between the U.S. and China", Reuters, July 2, 2019. [Google Scholar]

Radio Free Europe/Radio Liberty "Former Moldovan Lawmaker Sentenced to 14 Years for Spying for Russia." March 13, 2018. [Google Scholar]

Raik, K. "Liberalism and Geopolitics in EU–Russia Relations: Rereading the 'Baltic factor." European Security 25, no. 2 (2016): 237–255. doi:10.1080/09662

839.2016.1179628. [Taylor & Francis Online] [Web of Science ®], [Google Scholar]

Rathbone, J. P. "'on a Par with the Russians': Rise in Chinese Espionage Alarms Europe." Financial Times, August 30, 2022. [Google Scholar]

Reuters. "China Reported to Have Tried to Recruit Conservative German Lawmaker as Spy." July 6, 2018. [Google Scholar]

Reuters. "Retired German Political Scientist Charged with Spying for China." July 6, 2021. [Google Scholar]

Rogan, T. "France Spy Scandal Illustrates China's Growing Intelligence Challenge" The Washington Examiner, July 13, 2020. [Google Scholar]

Roonemaa, H. "How Smuggler Helped Russia to Catch Estonian Officer." Re:Baltica September 13, 2017. [Google Scholar]

Roonemaa, H. "Spiegs, ko Krievija aizmirsa." Re:Baltica, October 10, 2018. [Google Scholar]

Schindler, J. R. "Nato's Big New Russian Spy Scandal", Observer, May 25, 2016. [Google Scholar]

Shlapak, D., and M. Johnson. Deterrence on Nato's Eastern Flank: Wargaming the Defense of the Baltics, RR-1253-A. Santa Monica, CA: RAND, 2016. doi:10.7249/RR1253. [Crossref], [Google Scholar]

Silke, A. "The Devil You Know: Continuing Problems with Research on Terrorism." Terrorism and Political Violence 14, no. 4 (2001): 1–14. doi:10.1080/09546550109609697. [Taylor & Francis Online], [Google Scholar]

Springe, I. "How Latvia is (Not) Catching Russian Spies." Re:Baltica, May 17, 2018a. [Google Scholar]

Springe, I. "Uzdevums noskaidrot vai latvija ir Abrams tanki (smagie)?" Re:Baltica, November 22, 2018b. [Google Scholar]

SVT Nyheter. "Bröder döms för grovt spioneri." January 19, 2023. [Google Scholar]

SVT Nyheter. "FOI-forskaren om spionbröderna: Gjort väldigt stor skada." January 19, 2023. [Google Scholar]

Swedish Security Service. Säkerhetspolisen 2021. Stockholm, 2021. [Google Scholar]

Taylor, S. A., and D. Snow. "Cold War Spies: Why They Spied and How They Got Caught." Intelligence & National Security 12, no. 2 (1997): 101–125. doi:10.1080/02684529708432416. [Taylor & Francis Online], [Google Scholar]

Thompson, T. J. "Toward an Updated Understanding of Espionage Motivation." International Journal of Intelligence & CounterIntelligence 27, no. 1 (2014):

58–72. doi:10.1080/08850607.2014.842805. [Taylor & Francis Online], [Google Scholar]

Toda, M. "A Russian Spy's Manual: Send a Secret Message to the Strela-3 Satellite and Betray NATO Allies." Dennik N, October 11, 2020a. [Google Scholar]

Toda, M. "The Sweet Life of Russian Spies in Slovakia: Drunken Parties in the High Tatras and a Conspiracy Apartment in Bratislava", Dennik N, August 12, 2020b. [Google Scholar]

Weiss, M. "The Hero Who Betrayed His Country." Atlantic, June 29, 2019. [Google Scholar]

Widen, J. J. "The Wennerström Spy Case: A Western Perspective." Intelligence & National Security 21, no. 6 (2006): 931–958. doi:10.1080/02684520601046283. [Taylor & Francis Online], [Google Scholar]

Willoughby, I. "Uncertainty Over Whether Czech Accused of Spying for Russians Will Face Prosecution." Radio Prague International, September 16, 2022. [Google Scholar]

Wood, S., and M. F. Wiskoff. Americans Who Spied Against Their Country Since World War II, PERS-TR-92-005. Monterey CA: U.S. Dept. of Defence, 1992. May. [Google Sc

**Chapter 8: Political drivers of Muslim Youth Radicalisation in France: Religious Radicalism as a Response to Nativism. Max-Valentin Robert & Ayhan Kaya**

1. Quinn Mecham (2014) proposed a definition of Islamist organisations in accordance with their political goals: 'they seek to transform society', and 'want to change both individual and collective behaviour within society, which will lead to social change in key areas'. Accordingly, society 'should be more moral' in Islamic terms, 'meaning that people within society are more likely to live Islamic precepts in their daily lives and social interactions' (Mecham 2014, 24).

2. Data available on: https://www.insee.fr/fr/statistiques/4797578?sommai re=4928952.

3. In this study, we take the notion of radicalisation as a process that starts as the expression of socioeconomic, political, spatial and psychological deprivation in a similar vein to the ways in which it is explained in social movement's literature (Calhoun 2011; Della Porta 2014, 2018; Kaya and Bee, in this special Issue). Independently from its causes, McCauley and Moskalenko (2008, 428) conceptualise radicalisation as a set of 'change in beliefs, feelings, and action toward support and sacrifice for intergroup conflict'. Such a definitional effort is necessary to avoid an understanding of radicalisation as a 'magical approach of religious beliefs' in the case of self-identified Muslim youths in general (Truong 2017, 16).

4. In a part of the literature, extremism was conceptualised in relationship with the potentiality of violence (Kazmi 2022, 741; Adam-Troian, Tecmen, and Kaya 2021). Astrid Bötticher (2017, 74) also defines extremism by highlighting its violent dimension, and argues that extremists glorify violence as a conflict resolution mechanism and are opposed to the constitutional state, majority-based democracy, the rule of law, and human rights for all. Through this perspective, radicals are distinguished from extremists because they are not necessarily extreme and violent in their choice of means to achieve their goals (Bötticher 2017, 75). In this article, the notions of radicalism and extremism are being used as two different terms. The former is used in a way that does not necessarily correspond to violence, while the latter is used as a term that is linked to violence.

5. Trevi Group is known to be the origin of the police cooperation among the Member States of the EU, which began in 1976. 'Trevi' stands for Terrorism, Radicalism, Extremism, Violence, and Internationalism, and operated as an intergovernmental network of representatives from justice and home affairs ministries (König and Trauner 2021).

6. According to the 1st article of the above-mentioned law, 'In public schools, middle schools and high schools, the wearing of signs or clothing by which students ostensibly manifest a religious affiliation is prohibited'.

7. The 1st article of this law states 'No one may, in the public space, wear clothing intended to conceal his or her face'.

8. 'Burkini à Grenoble: Wauquiez déclare la guerre à Piolle', Le Point, 3 May 2022. https://www.lepoint.fr/politique/burkini-wauquiez-menace-de-couper-les-subventions-de-grenoble-03-05-2022–2474171_20.php. Accessed 18 July 2022.

9. When this interview was conducted (September 2020), Eric Zemmour had not yet entered the electoral field and therefore was not competing against the RN.

10. Zappi, S., D. Mariama, Olivier, F., and Soazig, Le Neve. 2021. 'Islamo-gauchisme: Frédérique Vidal suscite un tollé dans le monde universitaire et un malaise au sein de la majorité', Le Monde, 18 February 2021. https://www.lemonde.fr/politique/article/2021/02/18/polemique-sur-l-islamo-gauchisme-la-ministre-de-l-enseignement-superieur-recadree-par-l-executif-et-les-chercheurs_6070388_823448.html. Accessed 18 July 2022.

11. For more information about the murder of Samuel Paty, see 'Assassinat de Samuel Paty', France Info. Available on: https://www.francetvinfo.fr/faits-divers/terrorisme/enseignant-decapite-dans-les-yvelines/. Accessed 18 July 2022.

12. Rebeu: Arab/North African person in verlan slang.

13. CNews: private TV channel, ideologically close to the conservative and identitarian right. Sometimes described as a 'French-style Fox News', this channel is also accused of having promoted the ideological line of Eric Zemmour, who had a daily program on CNews before running for president in 2022.

## References

Adam-Troian, J., A. Tecmen, and A. Kaya. 2021. "Youth Extremism as a Response to Global Threats? A Threat-Regulation Perspective on Violent Extremism Among the Youth." European Psychologist 26 (1): 15–28. doi:10.1027/1016-9040/a000415. [Crossref], [Web of Science °], [Google Scholar]

Ahmed, S. 2017. What is Islam? The Importance of Being Islamic. Princeton, NJ: Princeton University Press. [Google Scholar]

Ali, M. 2018. Young Muslim America: Faith, Community, and Belonging. New York: Oxford University Press. [Crossref], [Google Scholar]

Allen, C. 2010. Islamophobia. Farnham, UK: Ashgate. [Google Scholar]

Azabar, S., and P. Thijssen. 2020. "Un examen approfondi des différences régionales dans le comportement électoral et les motifs de vote des musulmans." In Les électeurs locaux ont leurs préférences, edited by R. Dandoy, J. Dodeigne, K. Steyvers, and T. Verthé, 89–110. Bruges: Vanden Broele. [Google Scholar]

Bartlett, J., and C. Miller. 2012. "The Edge of Violence: Towards Telling the Difference Between Violent and Non-Violent Radicalisation." Terrorism and Political Violence 24 (1): 1–21. doi:10.1080/09546553.2011.594923. [Taylor & Francis Online], [Web of Science °], [Google Scholar]

Beaman, J. 2017. Citizen Outsider. Children of North African Immigrants in France. Berkeley: University of California Press. [Crossref], [Google Scholar]

Beekers, D., and L. Schrijvers. 2020. "Religion, Sexual Ethics, and the Politics of Belonging: Young Muslims and Christians in the Netherlands." Social Compass 67 (1): 137–156. doi:10.1177/0037768620901664. [Crossref], [Web of Science °], [Google Scholar]

Berntzen, L. E. 2020. Liberal Roots of Far Right Activism. The Anti-Islamic Movement in the 21st Century. Abingdon: Routledge. [Google Scholar]

Bisin, A., E. Patacchini, T. Verdier, and Y. Zenou. 2008. "Are Muslim Immigrants Different in Terms of Cultural Integration?" Journal of the European Economic Association 6 (2–3): 445–456. doi:10.1162/JEEA.2008.6.2-3.445. [Crossref], [Web of Science °], [Google Scholar]

Bötticher, A. 2017. "Towards Academic Consensus Definitions of Radicalism and Extremism." Perspectives on Terrorism 11 (4): 73–77. [Google Scholar]

Brouard, S., and V. Tiberj. 2005. Français comme les autres? Enquête sur les citoyens d'origine maghrébine, africaine et turque. Paris: Presses de Sciences Po. [Crossref], [Google Scholar]

Brown, K. E., and T. Saeed. 2015. "Radicalization and Counter-Radicalization at British Universities: Muslim Encounters and Alternatives." Ethnic and Racial Studies 38 (11): 1952–1968. [Taylor & Francis Online], [Web of Science ®], [Google Scholar]

Brubaker, R. 2017. "Between Nationalism and Civilizationism: The European Populist Moment in Comparative Perspective." Ethnic and Racial Studies 40 (8): 1191–1226. doi:10.1080/01419870.2017.1294700. [Taylor & Francis Online], [Web of Science ®], [Google Scholar]

Calhoun, C. 2011. The Roots of Radicalism: Tradition, the Public Sphere, and Early 19th Century Social Movements. Chicago: Chicago University Press. [Google Scholar]

Capelos, T., and N. Demertzis. 2018. "Political Action and Resentful Affectivity in Critical Times." Humanity & Society 42 (4): 410–433. doi:10.1177/0160597618802517. [Crossref], [Google Scholar]

Capelos, T., and A. Katsanidou. 2018. "Reactionary Politics: Explaining the Psychological Roots of Anti-Preferences in European Integration and Immigration Debates." Political Psychology 39 (6): 1271–1288. doi:10.1111/pops.12540. [Crossref], [Web of Science ®], [Google Scholar]

Cardenas, D. 2019. "Dual Identity, Minority Group Pressure, and the Endorsement of Minority Rights: A Study Among Sunni and Alevi Muslim in Western Europe." The Journal of Social Issues 75 (2): 592–610. doi:10.1111/josi.12328. [Crossref], [Web of Science ®], [Google Scholar]

Ciftci, S., F. M. Wuthrich, and A. Shamaileh. 2022. Religion, Social Relations, and Public Preferences in the Middle East and North Africa. Bloomington, Indiana: Indiana University Press. [Google Scholar]

Clifford, J. 1987. Predicament of Culture. Cambridge, MA: Harvard University Press. [Google Scholar]

Clifford, J. 1994. "Diasporas." Cultural Anthropology 9 (3): 302–338. doi:10.1525/can.1994.9.3.02a00040. [Crossref], [Web of Science ®], [Google Scholar]

Coolsaet, R. 2019. "Radicalization: The Origins and Limits of a Contested Concept." In Radicalization in Belgium and the Netherlands: Critical Perspectives on Violence and Security, edited by N. Fadil, M. de Koning, and F. Ragazzi, 29–51. London: I.B. Tauris. [Crossref], [Google Scholar]

Dargent, C. 2019. "Recul du catholicisme, croissance des non-affiliés et des minorités religieuses." In La France des valeurs. Quarante ans d'évolution, edited by P. Bréchon, F. Gonthier, and S. Astor, 228–233. Grenoble: Presses Universitaires de Grenoble. [Crossref], [Google Scholar]

De Certeau, M. 1984. The Practice of Everyday Life, edited by S. Rendall. Berkeley: University of California Press. [Google Scholar]

Del Grosso, M. O. 2015. "The Means and Issues Involved in Making Muslims Visible in France's Social and Political Space." Confluences Méditerranée 95 (4): 59–68. doi:10.3917/come.095.0059. [Crossref], [Google Scholar]

Della Porta, D. 2014. "On Violence and Repression: A Relational Approach (The Government and Opposition /Leonard Schapiro Memorial Lecture, 2013)." Government and Opposition 49 (2): 159–187. doi:10.1017/gov.2013.47. [Crossref], [Web of Science *], [Google Scholar]

Della Porta, D. 2018. "Radicalization: A Relational Perspective." Annual Review of Political Science 21 (1): 461–474. doi:10.1146/annurev-polis-ci-042716-102314. [Crossref], [Web of Science *], [Google Scholar]

Deltombe, T. 2007. L'islam imaginaire. La construction médiatique de l'islamophobie en France, 1975-2005. Paris: La Découverte. [Google Scholar]

Doerschler, P., and P. Irving Jackson. 2012. "Do Muslims in Germany Really Fail to Integrate? Muslim Integration and Trust in Public Institutions." Journal of International Migration and Integration 13 (4): 503–523. doi:10.1007/s12134-011-0220-6. [Crossref], [Google Scholar]

Doosje, B., A. Loseman, and K. Van Den Bos. 2013. "Determinants of Radicalization of Islamic Youth in the Netherlands: Personal Uncertainty, Perceived Injustice, and Perceived Group Threat." The Journal of Social Issues 69 (3): 586–604. doi:10.1111/josi.12030. [Crossref], [Web of Science *], [Google Scholar]

Edmunds, J. 2010. "'Elite Young Muslims in Britain: From Transnational to Global Politics." Contemporary Islam 4 (2): 215–238. doi:10.1007/s11562-009-0107-x. [Crossref], [Google Scholar]

Egger, C., and R. Magni-Berton. 2021. "The Role of Islamist Ideology in Shaping Muslim Believers' Attitudes Toward Terrorism: Evidence from Europe." Studies in Conflict & Terrorism 44 (7): 581–604. doi:10.1080/105761 0X.2019.1571696. [Taylor & Francis Online], [Google Scholar]

Eliade, M. 1991. Images and Symbols: Studies in Religious Symbolism. Princeton, New Jersey: Princeton University Press. [Google Scholar]

Fadil, N., and M. D. Koning. 2019. "Turning 'Radicalization' into Science: Ambivalent Translations into the Dutch (Speaking) Academic Field." In Radicalization in Belgium and the Netherlands, edited by N. Fadil, M. de Koning, and F. Ragazzi, 53–79. London: I.B.Tauris. [Crossref], [Google Scholar]

Fairclough, N. 1992. Discourse and Social Change. Cambridge: Polity Press. [Google Scholar]

Frisina, A. 2010. "Young Muslims' Everyday Tactics and Strategies: Resisting Islamophobia, Negotiating Italianness, Becoming Citizens." Journal of Intercultural Studies 31 (5): 557–572. doi:10.1080/07256868.2010.513087. [Taylor & Francis Online], [Google Scholar]

Galland, O. 2019. "Des musulmans plus religieux et plus traditionnels que les chrétiens." In La France des valeurs. Quarante ans d'évolution, edited by P. Bréchon, F. Gonthier, and S. Astor, 234–241. Grenoble: Presses Universitaires de Grenoble. [Crossref], [Google Scholar]

Gilroy, P. 1995. "Roots and Routes: Black Identity as an Outernational Project." In Racial and Ethnic Identity: Psychological Development and Creative Expression, edited by H. W. Harris, et al., 15–30. London: Routledge. [Google Scholar]

Gonthier, F., and T. Guerra. 2022. "From the People, Like the People, or for the People? Candidate Appraisal Among the French Yellow Vests." Political Psychology 43 (5): 969–989. doi:10.1111/pops.12826. [Crossref], [Web of Science *], [Google Scholar]

Guerra, T., C. Alexandre, and F. Gonthier. 2020. "Populist Attitudes Among the French Yellow Vests." Populism 3 (1): 1–12. doi:10.1163/25888072-02021039. [Crossref], [Google Scholar]

Gurr, T. R. 1969. Why Men Rebel. Princeton: Princeton University Press. [Google Scholar]

Hadjar, A., D. Schiefer, K. Boehnke, W. Frindte, and D. Geschke. 2019. "Devoutness to Islam and the Attitudinal Acceptance of Political Violence Among Young Muslims in Germany." Political Psychology 40 (2): 205–222. doi:10.1111/pops.12508. [Crossref], [Google Scholar]

Halliday, F. 1999. "Islamophobia Reconsidered." Ethnic and Racial Studies 22 (5): 892–902. doi:10.1080/014198799329305. [Taylor & Francis Online], [Web of Science *], [Google Scholar]

Haynes, J. 2021. "Religion in International Relations: Theory and Practice." In Handbook on Religion and International Relations, edited by J. Haynes, 5–23. Cheltenham: Edward Elgar Publishing. [Crossref], [Google Scholar]

Kabir, N. A. 2012. Young American Muslims. Dynamics of Identity. Edinburgh: Edinburgh University Press. [Crossref], [Google Scholar]

Kaya, A. 2009. Islam, Migration and Integration. The Age of Securitization. London: Palgrave Macmillan. [Crossref], [Google Scholar]

Kaya, A. 2012. "Transnational Citizenship: German-Turks and Liberalizing Citizenship Regimes." Citizenship Studies 16 (2): 153–172. doi:10.1080/13621025.2012.667608. [Taylor & Francis Online], [Web of Science *], [Google Scholar]

Kaya, A. 2015. "Islamophobism as an Ideology in the West: Scapegoating Muslim-Origin Migrants." In International Handbook of Migration and Social

Transformation in Europe, edited by A. Amelina, K. Horvath, and B. Meeus, 281–294. Berlin: Springer. [Google Scholar]

Kaya, A. 2021. "Islamist and Nativist Reactionary Radicalization in Europe." Politics and Governance 9 (3): 204–214. doi:10.17645/pag.v9i3.3877. [Crossref], [Google Scholar]

Kaya, A., and J. Adam-Troian. 2021. "Co-Radicalisation of Islamist and Nativist Extremists in Europe: A Social-Psychological and Sociological Perspective." Journal of Muslims in Europe 10 (3): 1–34. doi:10.1163/22117954-bja10034. [Crossref], [Google Scholar]

Kaya, A., and A. Drhimeur. 2022, July . "Diaspora Politics and Religious Diplomacy in Turkey and Morocco". Southeast European and Black Sea Studies 1–21. 10.1080/14683857.2022.2095703 [Taylor & Francis Online], [Google Scholar]

Kay, A. C., D. Gaucher, I. McGregor, and K. Nash. 2010. "Religious Belief as Compensatory Control." Personality and Social Psychology Review 14 (1): 37–48. doi:10.1177/1088868309353750. [Crossref], [PubMed], [Web of Science ®], [Google Scholar]

Kazmi, Z. 2022. "Radical Islam in the Western Academy." Review of International Studies 48 (4): 725–747. doi:10.1017/S0260210521000553. [Crossref], [Google Scholar]

Koenig, M. 2005. "Incorporating Muslim Migrants in Western Nation States – a Comparison of the United Kingdom, France, and Germany." Journal of International Migration and Integration / Revue de l'integration Et de la Migration Internationale 6 (2): 219–234. doi:10.1007/s12134-005-1011-8. [Crossref], [Google Scholar]

König, F., and F. Trauner. 2021. "From Trevi to Europol: Germany's Role in the Integration of EU Police Cooperation." Journal of European Integration 43 (2): 175–190. doi:10.1080/07036337.2021.1877694. [Taylor & Francis Online], [Web of Science ®], [Google Scholar]

Kranendonk, M., F. Vermeulen, and A. van Heelsum. 2018. ""Unpacking" the Identity-To-Politics Link: The Effects of Social Identification on Voting Among Muslim Immigrants in Western Europe." Political Psychology 39 (1): 43–67. doi:10.1111/pops.12397. [Crossref], [Web of Science ®], [Google Scholar]

Laclau, E., and C. Mouffe. 1985. Hegemony and Socialist Strategy: Towards a Radical Democratic Politics. London: Verso. [Google Scholar]

Lahnait, F. 2021. "La lucha contra la radicalización en Francia: de la experimentación a la profesionalización." Revista CIDOB d'Afers Internacionals 128 (128): 105–129. doi:10.24241/rcai.2021.128.2.105/en. [Crossref], [Google Scholar]

Lévi Straus, C. 1987. Introduction to the Work of Marcel Mauss. London: Routledge & Kegan Paul. [Google Scholar]

MacIntyre, A. 1971. Against the Self-Images of the Age: Essays on Ideology. New York: Schoken Books. [Google Scholar]

Manning, N., and P. Akhtar. 2020. "'No, We Vote for Whoever We Want to': Young British Muslims Making New Claims on Citizenship Amidst Ongoing Forms of Marginalisation." London School of Economics – British Politics and Policy 24 (7): 1–3. doi:10.1080/13676261.2020.1784855. [Taylor & Francis Online], [Google Scholar]

Marchal, R., and Z. O. Ahmed Salem. 2018. "La 'radicalisation' aide-t-elle à mieux penser?" Politique Africaine 149 (1): 5–20. doi:10.3917/polaf.149.0005. [Crossref], [Google Scholar]

Maskaliunaite, A. 2015. "Exploring the Theories of Radicalization." Interdisciplinary Political and Cultural Journal 17 (1): 9–26. doi:10.1515/ipcj-2015-0002. [Crossref], [Google Scholar]

Maxwell, R. 2010. "Trust in Government Among British Muslims: The Importance of Migration Status." Political Behavior 32 (1): 89–109. doi:10.1007/s11109-009-9093-1. [Crossref], [Web of Science *], [Google Scholar]

McCauley, C., and S. Moskalenko. 2008. "Mechanisms of Political Radicalization: Pathways Toward Terrorism." Terrorism and Political Violence 20 (3): 415–433. doi:10.1080/09546550802073367. [Taylor & Francis Online], [Web of Science *], [Google Scholar]

McDonald, L. Z. 2011. "Securing Identities, Resisting Terror: Muslim Youth Work in the UK and Its Implications for Security." Religion, State & Society 39 (2–3): 177–189. doi:10.1080/09637494.2011.584712. [Taylor & Francis Online], [Google Scholar]

Mecham, Q. 2014. "Islamist Parties as Strategic Actors: Electoral Participation and Its Consequences." In Islamist Parties and Political Normalization in the Muslim World, edited by Q. Mecham and J. Chernov-Hwang, 17–39. Philadelphia: University of Pennsylvania Press. [Crossref], [Google Scholar]

Nilan, P. 2017. Muslim Youth in the Diaspora. Challenging Extremism Through Popular Culture. Abingdon: Routledge. [Crossref], [Google Scholar]

Obaidi, M., R. Bergh, J. Sidanius, and L. Thomsen. 2018. "The Mistreatment of My People: Victimization by Proxy and Behavioral Intentions to Commit Violence Among Muslims in Denmark." Political Psychology 39 (3): 577–593. doi:10.1111/pops.12435. [Crossref], [Web of Science *], [Google Scholar]

O'brien, J. 2018. Keeping It Halal: The Everyday Lives of Muslim American Teenage Boys. Princeton: Princeton University Press. [Crossref], [Google Scholar]

Orehek, E., and A. Vazeou-Nieuwenhuis. 2014. "Understanding the Terrorist Threat: Policy Implications of a Motivational Account of Terrorism." Policy Insights from the Behavioral and Brain Sciences 1 (1): 248–255. doi:10.1177/2372732214549747. [Crossref], [Google Scholar]

Powell, K. A. 2018. "Framing Islam/Creating Fear: An Analysis of U.S. Media Coverage of Terrorism from 2011–2016." Religions 9 (9): 1–15. doi:10.3390/rel9090257. [Crossref], [Google Scholar]

Rigouste, M. 2012. La domination policière. Une violence industrielle. Paris: La fabrique éditions. [Google Scholar]

Roché, S., S. Astor, and Ö. Bilen. 2020. "Sentiment national : un clivage entre adolescents irréligieux et musulmans." In Indifférence religieuse ou athéisme militant? Penser l'irréligion aujourd'hui, edited by P. Bréchon and A.-L. Zwilling, 99–115. Grenoble: Presses Universitaires de Grenoble. [Google Scholar]

Schmid, A. P. 2013. "Radicalisation, de-Radicalisation, Counter-Radicalisation: A Conceptual Discussion and Literature Review." ICCT Research Paper 97 (1). doi:10.19165/2013.1.02. [Crossref], [Google Scholar]

Seurat, L. 2020. "Partir à La Mecque. Mobilités et appartenances de la jeunesse musulmane française." In Désirs d'Islam. Portraits d'une minorité religieuse en France, edited by L. Bucaille, 57–80. Paris: Presses de Sciences Po. [Crossref], [Google Scholar]

Tiberj, V. 2020. "The Muslims next door. Portraits d'une minorité religieuse française." In Désirs d'Islam. Portraits d'une minorité religieuse en France, edited by L. Bucaille, 35–55. Paris: Presses de Sciences Po. [Crossref], [Google Scholar]

Tilly, C. 1978. "From Mobilization to Revolution." CRSO Working Paper, 156. New York: Random House. [Google Scholar]

Tilly, C. 2003. The Politics of Collective Violence. Cambridge, MA: Cambridge University Press. [Crossref], [Google Scholar]

Truong, F. 2017. Loyautés radicales. L'islam et les "mauvais garçons" de la nation. Paris: La Découverte. [Google Scholar]

Verkuyten, M., and A. Yildiz. 2007. "National (Dis)identification and Ethnic and Religious Identity: A Study Among Turkish-Dutch Muslims." Personality & Social Psychology Bulletin 33 (10): 1448–1462. doi:10.1177/0146167207304276. [Crossref], [PubMed], [Web of Science ®], [Google Scholar]

Villechaise, A., and L. Bucaille. 2020. "Jeunes femmes musulmanes. Lutter contre la domination via l'islam." In Désirs d'Islam. Portraits d'une minorité religieuse en France, edited by L. Bucaille, 133–171. Paris: Presses de Sciences Po. [Crossref], [Google Scholar]

Zegnani, S. 2018. "Les carrières des jeunes salafis des quartiers populaires : entre radicalité et conformisme." Agora débats/jeunesses 80 (3): 117–131. doi:10.3917/agora.080.0117. [Crossref], [Google Scholar]

Zolberg, A. R. 2004. "The Democratic Management of Cultural Differences: Building Inclusive Societies in Western Europe and North America." Occasional Paper. New York: United Nations Development Programme [Google Scholar]

# Index

# W

Wagner militia  1, 14

World War I  33

# Y

Yellow Vests  i, iii, 1, 2, 5, 15, 35, 43, 49,
50, 108, 134, 157

# About the Author

Musa Khan Jalalzai is a journalist and research scholar. He has written extensively on Afghanistan, terrorism, nuclear and biological terrorism, human trafficking, drug trafficking, and intelligence research and analysis. He was an Executive Editor of the Daily Outlook Afghanistan from 2005-2011, and a permanent contributor in Pakistan's daily *The Post*, *Daily Times*, and *The Nation*, *Weekly the Nation*, (London). However, in 2004, US Library of Congress in its report for South Asia mentioned him as the biggest and prolific writer. He received Masters in English literature, Diploma in Geospatial Intelligence, University of Maryland, Washington DC, certificate in Surveillance Law from the University of Stanford, USA, and diploma in Counter terrorism from Pennsylvania State University, California, the United States.

Milton Keynes UK
Ingram Content Group UK Ltd.
UKHW040855181023
430815UK00003B/16